No stranger in the city

No stranger in the city

God's concern for urban people

Ian Coffey
George McKinney
Ray Bakke
Floyd McClung
Harvie M. Conn
Luis Palau
Peter Maiden
Ajith Fernando

Inter-Varsity Press
STL Books

INTER-VARSITY PRESS
38 De Montfort Street, Leicester LE1 7GP, England

Articles, with the exception of those by Ian Coffey, Peter Maiden and
the Foreword by Roger Forster, previously appeared in *Confessing
Christ as Lord: The Urbana '81 Compendium, Faithful Witness:
Urbana '84,* and *Urban Mission: God's concern for the city,* all
published by IVP of the USA. Used by permission. Chapter 6,
'Concern for the masses,' is copyright © 1985 by Luis Palau and used
by permission. Unless otherwise stated, Scripture quotations in this
publication are from the Holy Bible, New International Version.
Copyright © 1973, 1978, 1984 International Bible Society.
Published by Hodder & Stoughton.

First published in this form 1989

British Library Cataloguing in Publication Data
Coffey, Ian
No stranger in the city.
1. Urban regions. Christian church. Evangelism
I. Title
269'.2'09.732

ISBN 0-85110-848-2

Set in Linotron Century Schoolbook. Typeset in Great Britain by
Parker Typesetting Service, Leicester. Printed in Great Britain by
Cox & Wyman Ltd, Reading.

*Inter-Varsity Press is the book-publishing division of the Universities
and Colleges Christian Fellowship (formerly the Inter-Varsity
Fellowship), a student movement linking Christian Unions in
universities and colleges throughout the United Kingdom and the
Republic of Ireland, and a member movement of the International
Fellowship of Evangelical Students. For information about local and
national activities write to UCCF, 38 De Montfort Street,
Leicester LE1 7GP.*

*Published jointly with STL Books. STL Books are published by Send
the Light (Operation Mobilisation), PO Box 48, Bromley, Kent,
BR1 3JH.*

CONTENTS

Part II: A Bible exposition

FOREWORD

I have been very pleased to read this book. It is my necessary and happy duty to commend its message; it would have been irresponsible of me to do otherwise.

In the past five or six years I have noticed – and often remarked on the fact – that young people are moving back into the cities for Christ's sake. When I was first in Christian ministry the trend was almost exclusively in the opposite direction. Trained ministers and leaders looked for pastorates and positions in the suburbs and rural areas. This left the city – particularly the inner heart of the city – without an evangelistic presence. The wind of change (indeed the wind of the Spirit), however, has reversed this trend. Each year we have the thrill of seeing increased numbers of young people training with us in order to feel their way into long-term committed service in inner-city work. Other movements and societies such as city missions report the same trend.

God is, I believe, in this current spiritual concern. I believe too, however, that he was in the emergence of the cosmopolitan cities. The European church took a long time to reach and evangelize the Vikings. God used their murderous raids round the British Isles, Spain, the Mediterranean, through the Black Sea into Russia. They were evangelized through the Christian wives they stole while on these excursions. In a similar way the British Empire – 'on which the sun never sets' – was too often the authority which prohibited evangelism, while offering a good opportunity to spread the message of Jesus. Subsequently God has brought the nations of the earth to Britain to give us a second chance.

Racism and cultural identities may harden in our cosmopolitan cities. But this melting-pot ethos, never found in rural conditions, is ideal for expressing the one new humanity of Christ where 'There is neither Jew nor Greek, slave nor free, male nor female' (Galatians 3:28). We need such church communities, which reflect this new humanity, to be witnesses of the good news of the kingdom to the nations before Jesus comes again. Cities are a huge mass congregation gathered together by God for evangelization. There are many deprived and discouraged humans in inner-city circumstances who will best understand and respond to our gospel which is tailored for the poor.

Spiritual forces of the city lie behind the authorities and so often are found embodied in the social structures of the city. The apostle Paul calls these 'the spiritual principalities and powers'. I would have liked to have found more in the book concerning them. No doubt, however, this book is an appetizer of good things yet to come.

Our future is a city – the city of God. Let us prepare for it by redeeming as many of our present ones as we can!

Roger Forster
Ichthus Team Ministries

1
INTRODUCTION: NO STRANGER IN THE CITY

IAN COFFEY

What made the first Christians world-changers?
We read in the book of Acts that the charge was
laid against two of their number that 'these men ...
have turned the world upside down' (Acts 17:6,
RSV). In the space of a few years the Christian message had spread around the known world like a
raging forest fire. Small in number, poor in resources, lacking political power or influence – the followers of Jesus of Nazareth achieved remarkable
success.

Michael Green has commented on this accom-
plishment:

It was a small group of eleven men whom Jesus
commissioned to carry on his work, and bring the

gospel to the whole world. They were not distinguished; they were not well educated; they had no influential backers. In their own nation they were nobodies and, in any case, their own nation was a mere second-class province on the eastern extremity of a Roman map. If they had stopped to weigh up the probabilities of succeeding in their mission, even granted their conviction that Jesus was alive and that his Spirit went with them to equip them for their task, their hearts must surely have sunk, so heavily were the odds weighted against them. How could they possibly succeed? And yet they did.

(*Evangelism in the Early Church*, Highland Books, 1984)

How did they do it? The Bible provides several answers to our question. First and foremost their success lay not in their own abilities but the power of the Holy Spirit. Jesus had promised: 'But you will receive power when the Holy Spirit comes on you; and you will be my witnesses in Jerusalem, and in all Judea and Samaria, and to the ends of the earth' (Acts 1:8). Secondly, they were committed people. They were committed to Jesus of Nazareth in the belief that he was the crucified, risen and ascended Messiah, the Son of God and the Saviour of the world. The first leaders of the church were eyewitnesses of the resurrection – it was a condition that you could not be an apostle unless you had seen the risen Jesus personally. They were committed to making Jesus the Christ known to others – regardless of the cost to themselves. Persecution, even death, did not quench their evangelistic enthusiasm.

A third clue to their success lies in their approach to spreading the Christian 'good news'. They were strategists when it came to evangelism. The book of Acts tells of two basic types of evangelism – the spontaneous and the planned.

An example of spontaneous evangelism is seen in the encounter between a royal official from Ethiopia and Philip – one of the first Christians (Acts 8:26–40). Luke (who wrote the book of Acts) points out that an 'angel of the Lord' directed Philip to the desert road for the unplanned meeting with the Ethiopian. It was the Holy Spirit, according to Luke, who prompted Philip to engage the stranger in a conversation which led to his conversion.

This incident is one of several in Acts where no human pre-planning was involved. God was at work, preparing the ground and moving his troops into position. The initiative was divine, not human. Little wonder it has often been remarked that a more accurate title for the book would be 'The Acts of the Holy Spirit' – rather than 'The Acts of the Apostles'.

I have termed the other type of evangelism we read of in Acts – the planned. Barnabas and Saul (later Paul) were sent out on a journey from their church in Antioch. Their trip resulted in the planting of several churches in other parts of Asia. It was the first of a number of such towns where there was a definite objective in view – to preach the good news of Jesus Christ. But even in planned evangelism, the direction of the Holy Spirit is paramount. He initiated the decision taken by the church at Antioch and later, in his missionary travels, Paul refers to the Holy Spirit's intervention in his planning (Acts 13:1ff.; 16:1–10).

13

We are called to reach our twentieth-century world for Christ and we would do well to learn some lessons from our first-century sisters and brothers. Spirit-directed evangelism is needed, both spontaneous and planned.

In contrast to the poverty and powerlessness of the first Christians, we seem to have so much. The western church has much in terms of resources, but that in itself is the cause of our weakness. We have become over-dependent on things rather than on God, confident in our own abilities rather than relying on his. Like the church at Laodicea we boast in our riches instead of bemoaning our spiritual poverty. Christ stands 'outside of us' asking to be invited back to the central place he deserves (Revelation 3:14–22). It is in repentance that we discover the power source once again.

Open your eyes

Spirit-directed evangelism is more than the bare acknowledgment of our need of his help in making Jesus known. We need him to show us the world from God's perspective, to melt our hearts to share the feeling God has for men and women, to inspire our prayers and to reveal to us a strategy for reaching our generation for Christ.

There are some who take the view that 'urban evangelism' (the shorthand phrase that means making Jesus known in the cities) is just the latest fad in the changing fashions of Christianity. I do not believe that for a moment. The stirring in the hearts of God's people about the cities of our world has come about because God's heart is stirred by them too.

Jesus urged his disciples to 'Open your eyes and

look at the fields!' (John 4:35). When you start to look at the world through God's eyes, you take the first step towards Spirit-directed evangelism. Concern for the cities of the world is not the 'latest thing' in evangelism, but comes from a godly understanding of today's (and tomorrow's) world.

There are three reasons why cities are of strategic importance in the advance of the Kingdom of God.

1. *Cities are population centres.* All over the world cities are growing. That growth is not measured simply in terms of concrete and steel but by the explosion of growth in population. The following table was produced by Ray Bakke, one of the contributors to this book. It appeared as part of an article in the magazine *World Evangelization*. It shows the top 30 cities of the world with their estimated populations in the years 1990 and 2000. As you reflect on the staggering proposition that by the end of the century Mexico City will be home to 26.3 million people and Sao Paulo will have a population of 24 million – put alongside those figures the current population of a nation such as Greece with 10 million people, Australia with 16 million or Canada with 25 million. The fact that we now have cities which are larger than nations is sufficient for them to become the focus of our attention. Populations are people and God's heart concern is for people, wherever they may be found.

2. *Cities are entry points.* Paul knew the value of using a city as an entry point for the gospel. That is why he invested two years of his life by staying in the city of Ephesus and preaching daily in a secular lecture hall. Paul knew that Ephesus was a busy seaport and trading-centre and could become a

The World's Largest Agglomerations, 1990–2000

Rank	Agglomeration/Country	Pop. in 1990	Agglomeration/Country	Pop. in 2000
1	Mexico City, Mexico	21.3	Mexico City, Mexico	26.3
2	São Paulo, Brazil	18.1	São Paulo, Brazil	24.0
3	Tokyo/Yokohama, Japan	17.2	Tokyo/Yokohama, Japan	17.1
4	NY/North-Eastern NJ, USA	15.3	Calcutta, India	16.6
5	Calcutta, India	12.6	Greater Bombay, India	16.0
6	Shanghai, China	12.0	NY/North-Eastern NJ, USA	15.5
7	Greater Bombay, India	11.9	Seoul, Republic of Korea	13.5
8	Greater Buenos Aires, Argentina	11.7	Shanghai, China	13.5
9	Seoul, Republic of Korea	11.5	Rio de Janeiro, Brazil	13.3
10	Rio de Janeiro, Brazil	11.4	Delhi, India	13.3
11	L.A./Long Beach, USA	10.5	Greater Buenos Aires, Argentina	13.2
12	Cairo/Giza/Imbaba, Egypt	10.0	Cairo/Giza/Imbaba, Egypt	13.2
13	London, United Kingdom	9.5	Jakarta, Indonesia	12.8
14	Beijing (Peking) China	9.5	Baghdad, Iraq	12.8
15	Jakarta, Indonesia	9.3	Teheran, Iran	12.7
16	Moscow, U.S.S.R	9.2	Karachi, Pakistan	12.2
17	Delhi, India	9.2	Istanbul, Turkey	11.9
18	Rhein-Ruhr, Federal Republic of Germany	9.1	L.A./Long Beach, USA	11.2
19	Paris, France	9.0	Dacca, Bangladesh	11.2
20	Teheran, Iran	9.0	Manila, Philippines	11.1
21	Baghdad, Iraq	8.9	Beijing (Peking), China	10.8

The World's Largest Agglomerations, 1990–2000

Rank	Agglomeration/Country	Pop. in 1900	Agglomeration/Country	Pop. in 2000
22	Istanbul, Turkey	8.4	Moscow, U.S.S.R	10.1
23	Manila, Philippines	8.3	Bangkok/Thonburi, Thailand	9.5
24	Karachi, Pakistan	8.2	Tianjin, China	9.2
25	Tianjin, China	8.0	Paris, France	9.2
26	Osaka/Koba, Japan	7.8	Lima–Callo, Peru	9.1
27	Milan, Italy	7.3	London, United Kingdom	9.1
28	Chicago/North-Western Indiana, USA	6.9	Kinshasa, Zaire	8.9
29	Lima-Caao, Peru	6.8	Rhein-Ruhr, Federal Republic of Germany	8.6
30	Dacca, India	6.5	Lagos, Nigeria	8.3

Statistics taken from *World Evangelization*, Vol. 15, No. 54, 1988.

gateway to reaching people far beyond the city boundaries. The wisdom of Paul's strategy is seen in Luke's summary of the long-stay approach, 'all the Jews and Greeks who lived in the province of Asia heard the word of the Lord.' Paul realized that in reaching a city he could reach a whole province. We too need to identify the key cities of our world which provide entry points for the gospel.

3. Cities have become no-go areas. When the current troubles flared up in Northern Ireland in the late 1960s, the phrase 'no-go area' became a part of everyday English vocabulary. When a street or housing estate was taken over by a mob, the police and military stayed away. The mob ruled and a no-go area became a place where the forces of law and order were powerless.

It is a disturbing fact that many of the world's cities have become no-go areas for the Christian church. City-centre churches, if they exist at all, have often been left to decay on the beach as the church-going-population tide has turned and receded to the suburbs. In the UK, where I live, city-centre churches are often huge, crumbling mausoleums with an elderly, dwindling congregation.

Cities breed crime and violence. Usually they are home to the poorest members of a society who live in overcrowded conditions. For these and other reasons, cities are unappealing to 'nice' people. This is in complete contrast to the Spirit-directed strategy of the first Christians. The evils of Ephesus, Corinth or Rome were not seen as barriers to the gospel. No-go areas simply did not exist for a man like Paul who believed that 'where sin increased, grace increased all the more,' (Romans 5:20).

18

A strategy for the cities

It is apparent that God is stirring his church for a new chapter in her history – perhaps the last. 'All over the world God's Spirit is moving' is not a cliche but a fact. Church-growth analysts tell us that the church worldwide is growing faster than at any other time in history. The Christian community in South Korea has more than doubled in the past 10 years and the church in China now numbers around 50 million. The church in Africa is growing at the astonishing rate of 16,400 people per day and 1,200 new churches are established around the world every week.

As an important part of this global harvest, God is raising up men and women with a vision to reach the cities of the world. John Scott has commented, 'Vision begins with a holy discontent with things as they are.' This holy discontent centres on the conviction that Jesus should not be a stranger in the city and that we, his people, must reclaim the ground from which we have retreated.

How can we reach the cities of the world with the gospel? This book seeks to put forward some answers to this question within a biblical framework. Our God is a God of infinite variety whose ways cannot be confined to a blueprint. What this book does is to lay down some principles, personal experiences and ideas alongside each other. Others will have to take and mix them with their own.

I want to put forward five ingredients for the mix which I believe to be essential, whatever the shape and colour of our Spirit-directed strategy.

1. Presence. To reach a city we must become part of it. The incarnation is a model for us in this respect because Jesus 'became flesh and made his dwelling among us' (John 1:14). He identified with us by becoming one with us. The cities will not be taken by forays from the suburbs. If God is calling us to reach the city-dwellers we need to become their next-door neighbours.

I remember working with a city-centre church which was surrounded by high-rise apartment blocks. The congregation was small but dedicated. In spite of years of faithful prayer, visitations and special projects, they had made little impact on their community. They were seen by the community as 'outsiders' who drove into the area in their cars a couple of times each week and after a few hours, drove straight out again. The church gradually began to face the challenge that they needed to move in and live alongside those they were trying to win to Christ.

2. Prayer. We need to pray for the cities of the world. This is the constant message that is coming from the many prayer-movements that have sprung up around the world in recent years. Urgent spiritual warfare is called for to dislodge the spiritual principalities and powers that rule over our cities (see Ephesians 6:12). We need to pray for our cities and in our cities, by taking prayer into the difficult neighbourhoods and centres of power and influence. In Britain, we have seen a large number of prayer marches in strategic cities over the past few years. These are not publicity exercises for the church or a new style of open-air evangelism (although people are made aware of the gospel through them) but principally they are a cry to God for mercy and deliverance, and a declaration against the hosts of darkness that hold power in the heavenly realms.

3. Proclamation. We need to preach Jesus in our cities. Mention preaching to most Christians and they immediately think of that rather obscure art form that has become almost deified in some churches. Mention preaching to the first Christians and it meant only one thing – telling the good news about Jesus Christ. Teaching was for insiders (Christians), preaching was for outsiders (the unconverted).

One of the reasons the early church grew so quickly as it did is that for 200 years they had no church buildings! Unable to gather in a ghetto, their Christian life and witness had to be earthed in the community in which they lived.

We need to be godly innovaters if we are going to reach large city populations with the gospel. We must break down the barriers of Christian culture that prevent us effectively communicating the message of Christ in a language that people can understand. We need to be risk-takers who are not afraid to make mistakes.

To cite just one example, John Wesley had to undergo a revolution in his own thinking as God began to show him, through the example of George Whitfield, the need to take the gospel to the people. He wrote in his *Journal*:

I could scarce reconcile myself at first to this strange way of preaching in the fields, of which he (George Whitfield) set me an example on Sunday; having been all my life (till very lately) as tenacious of every point relating to decency and order, that I should have thought the saving of souls almost a sin if it had not been done in a church.

Roy Joslin, writing in his book *Urban Harvest* (Evangelical Press, 1982) lists the places where Wesley used to preach the good news about Jesus to men and women of his own generation:

He preached in a meat market, a corn market, a butter market, a shooting-range, a forge, a brick-yard, a bowling green, a malt-room, a room over a pigsty and a barn. He visited prisons, workhouses, hospitals and asylums. Much of his indoor preaching was done in private houses.

Wesley during his life travelled over a quarter of a million miles, preached 40,000 sermons and wrote over 200 books. Both he and Whitfield were used by God to reach thousands of ordinary people for Christ – often to the loud criticism of the religious establishment of their day. They were innovative risk-takers and that is what we need to be if we are going to reach the cities with the life-changing message of Jesus Christ.

4. Power. We need a fresh outpouring of the Holy Spirit if we are going to see God's Kingdom extended in the cities. Much has been written in recent years about 'power evangelism' and the need for 'signs and wonders' in evangelism today. This is not the place to evaluate the arguments in the light of Scripture and experience. But I do believe that most Christians would agree that for all our words, prayers, conferences, seminars and books – we know little of the Holy Spirit's power in our lives.

Increasingly we are seeing that cities are centres for evil. People who live in them are bound by sin and addictions, and the power of the Spirit is needed if we are going to see them delivered and converted. Cities are also places of alienation, injustice, poverty and deep personal needs. The power of the Spirit is required for compassion and acts of righteousness. After all, 'the Kingdom of God is not a matter of talk but of power' (1 Corinthians 4:20).

5. Planting. We must see Christian congregations planted in our cities. Preaching is part of evangelism, not the whole. Three hours in the open-air with a sketchboard is not, by itself, going to achieve the coming of the Kingdom of God in a city. We must help new Christians grow in their faith and become firmly established in Christ. Evangelism and discipling are inseparably bound together in the New Testament and we separate them at our peril.

But city people do not always conform to our tidy church patterns, which often, incidentally, are more a result of our culture than our theology. A pastor in a city-centre church recently told me of the way in which he has totally restructured his congregational life, in order to cope with the drug addicts, prostitutes and dossers who had come to faith in Christ. He found they could not fit into the church patterns and so he had started a cluster of discipleship groups based in homes around the city centre. The new Christians began to grow rapidly in an environment that was totally suited to their needs.

However God directs, we must see our evangelism in the cities giving birth to established congregations under caring leadership.

About this book

Most of the chapters in this book were originally delivered as addresses at recent Urbana student missions' conventions. Urbana is held every three years in the United States with the particular aim of challenging and informing Christian students about the needs of world mission.

The writers have between them a wealth of experience about evangelism in the cities of the world and I am sure you will find their insights helpful. All of us are children of our family background, culture and experiences and the way in which such things shape our thinking will be apparent from these pages. But it is our hope that you will find your heart stirred and your vision increased.

At its heart, this book has one central conviction. God loves the cities of our world and it is his desire that his Son, our Saviour, Jesus Christ should be no longer a stranger in the city.

IAN COFFEY

Ian Coffey is the Field Director for the Evangelical Alliance of Great Britain, and author of several books. An ordained Baptist Minister, he worked as a pastor for some years in the south of England. He was a founding Trustee of the Saltmine Trust, an interdenominational evangelistic team. As their Director of Evangelism, he worked as an evangelist in many parts of Britain and other parts of the world. He is married to Ruth and they have four young sons.

PART I
INTO THE CITY

George McKinney
Ray Bakke
Floyd McClung
Harvie M. Conn
Luis Palau
Peter Maiden

2
WITH CHRIST IN THE CITY

GEORGE McKINNEY

A careful perusal of holy history reveals that God has an unending love affair with the city. From the biblical record of the building of the first organized population centre by Cain, which he named after his son Enoch (Gn. 4:17), to the building of planned cities in our own day, God's concern and love for the city is evident. In spite of the historical evidence that cities have been the scene of mankind's greatest sin of arrogance, pride and rebellion against God, both the New and Old Testaments affirm that God unhesitatingly seeks to redeem the city and its inhabitants.

Abraham's plea for God's mercy on wicked Sodom would have been granted if only ten righteous persons could have been found. The great city of

Nineveh was spared when Jonah delivered God's message to its king who led that city-state in repentance. Nehemiah, under God's anointing, left the high position of cup-bearer to King Artaxerxes in Persia to lead a discouraged, defeated and disunified Jewish remnant in Jerusalem to rebuild the walls and to restore the city from ruins.

In the gospels Jesus made the public announcement of the beginning of his ministry in the synagogue in the city of Nazareth. His first recorded miracle was in the city of Cana of Galilee. While much of the work was done among the rural folk who heard him gladly, he nevertheless was a familiar figure in the temple in Jerusalem and the synagogue and streets of the cities of Caesarea, Jericho, Bethany, Capernaum and Bethesda. It was in the city that Jesus met his greatest opposition. He wept openly because of the injustice, oppression and sins of the city of Jerusalem. After his arrest, he was taken to the city hall and tried before Pilate. His vicarious and redemptive death occurred just outside the city walls. After his resurrection, he returned to the city and appeared to five hundred astounded citizens. Jesus directed the disciples to return to the city of Jerusalem and to wait there for the promised infilling of the Holy Ghost, and instructed them to begin their ministry in the city. And from the city, they were to reach the world.

Cities today

The reported death of God in the cities of the world is a false report. Those of us involved in ministry in the city can testify that in the city, as everywhere else, where sin abounds, there grace much more abounds:

Christ, the Wounded Healer, is present in the concrete jungles, in the overcrowded, rat- and roach-infested projects, in the halls of justice and in the prisons. As our eternal contemporary, he is wherever there is human hurt and suffering. Since God in Christ has never forsaken the city, neither must the church.

A careful examination of the urban scene reveals that the church and all social institutions are both challenged and threatened by conditions which are widespread in the twentieth-century West. These conditions, though observable because of physical manifestations, are primarily spiritual and theological. They are basically problems arising because of mankind's rebellion and alienation from God, and our pride, selfishness and contempt for others.

In recent years the church too often has been in captivity to society for economic and social reasons, and has not been free to fulfil its prophetic role of pronouncing judgment as well as proclaiming the way of healing and salvation. Rather, the church has too often simply reflected the prevailing social or political attitudes and values, and has said by its silence and complicity that majority and might make right. Consequently, the church in many cities of the world has lost its effective witness.

The city was the first laboratory for the testing of the power of the gospel to create a fellowship of love and forgiveness that cut across racial, language and socio-economic barriers. The success of the experiment is well-documented in the book of Acts. The Jerusalem church was multi-racial and multi-cultural. Christians from Africa, Asia and Europe sat at the communion table together and had 'all things in common.' It may be that much of the distress in our western cities is due to their abandonment by the many representatives of Christ, leaving only a remnant of his followers to do what Christ has commissioned all of us to do together.

Social diagnosticians, demographers and prophets of doom have researched the city and its problems, and they have all concluded that the major western cities are in a serious state of decay. The diagnosis generally includes information that:

1. Great population shifts have resulted in loss of tax bases and the concentration of poor and ethnic minorities in the city.

2. Modern technology has rendered many old skills and jobs obsolete and created need for new skills and professions.

3. Automation and robots are replacing people, without concern for their future livelihood. Thus many people are rendered obsolete.

4. Environmental pollution is worsening (air itself is poisoned and hazardous).

5. The criminal justice system has broken down before increased crime, violence and lawlessness.

6. The delivery of necessary social services to the poor and the defenceless has broken down.

7. The educational system is breaking down, resulting in schools that do not teach.

8. There are other demographic changes: (a) a growing percentage of older people in the total population, and (b) a growing youth population without skills.

In addition to this socio-economic diagnosis of the urban problems, we must add a spiritual analysis.

The city is the scene of spiritual confusion. Cults and non-biblical religions have proliferated, often led by opportunists and spiritual pimps who capitalize on the ignorance, spiritual hunger and vulnerability of many city dwellers who have never heard the gospel of Jesus Christ. Moreover, there are those in the city, like their counterparts in suburbia, who heard the gospel but rejected its claims on their lives. Consequently, God's wrath is revealed against those who renounced his grace. Paul gives a clear statement of the spiritual conditions in the major cities of the West today:

The wrath of God is being revealed from heaven against all the godlessness and wickedness of men who suppress the truth by their wickedness, since what may be known about God is plain to them, because God has made it plain to them. For since the creation of the world God's invisible qualities – his eternal power and divine nature – have been clearly seen, being understood from what has been made, so that men are without excuse. For although they knew God, they neither glorified him as God nor gave thanks to him, but their thinking became futile and their foolish hearts were darkened. Although they claimed to be wise, they became fools and exchanged the glory of the immortal God for images made to look like mortal man and birds and animals and reptiles. Therefore God gave them over in the sinful desires of their hearts to sexual impurity for the degrading of their bodies with one another. They exchanged the truth of God for a lie, and worshipped and served created things rather than the Creator –

who is for ever praised. Amen. Because of this, God gave them over to shameful lusts. Even their women exchanged natural relations for unnatural ones. In the same way the men also abandoned natural relations with women and were inflammed with lust for one another. Men committed indecent acts with other men, and received in themselves the due penalty for their perversion. Furthermore, since they did not think it worth while to retain the knowledge of God, he gave them over to a depraved mind, to do what ought not to be done. They have become filled with every kind of wickedness, evil, greed and depravity. They are full of envy, murder, strife, deceit and malice. They are gossips, slanderers, God-haters, insolent, arrogant and boastful; they invent ways of doing evil; they disobey their parents; they are senseless, faithless, heartless, ruthless. Although they know God's righteous decree that those who do such things deserve death, they not only continue to do these things but also approve of those who practise them. (Rom. 1:18–32)

The biblical diagnosis of the spiritual climate in the city is also the correct diagnosis of that of suburbia. God is no respecter of persons. When the person with power, wealth and prestige rejects the lordship of Christ and the authority of God's Word, the personal, social and spiritual results are the same as when a person without power, wealth and prestige rejects Christ. The Bible says God sends strong delusions on both the rich and the poor, the minority and the majority. The powerful and the powerless believe lies and are damned.

Please note that the wealthy who reject Christ and the poor who reject Christ believe the same lie – that gain (wealth) is godliness. Greed and covetousness motivate both. When the godless, poor and greedy become godless, middle class and greedy, their behaviour is hardly distinguishable from the old-line godless, rich and greedy. Thus, we conclude that the mere shifting of wealth from one segment or group in the society to another is not the solution to the problem of poverty in the city. There must be a spiritual change in the heart and consciousness – a new birth wrought by God that brings a new philosophy of wealth ('The earth is the Lord's and everything in it,' Ps. 24:1) and a new understanding of stewardship ('From everyone who has been given much, much will be demanded; and from the one who has been entrusted with much, much more will be asked', Lk. 12:48). Those who have wealth and power are stewards, accountable to God for its responsible use and distribution. Believing this, we issue a Macedonian call to our brothers and sisters who fled the city, 'Come back and help us.'

A second lie that many urbanites and suburbanites believe is that God has forsaken or abandoned the city. The poor, powerless and disinherited demonstrate that they believe God is gone from the city through their criminal behaviour, hopelessness, ruthlessness, murder, suicide, drug and alcohol addiction, abandonment of families, trafficking in human flesh, and the loss of reverence for all life and truth.

While powerless unbelieving urbanites tend to turn in upon themselves and resort to self-destructive behaviour, powerful unbelieving suburbanites tend to deify themselves and give greater value and worth to their property and power than to the life of the poor. Thus, they fail to use political and economic power to deal compassionately and creatively with the problems of the inner city.

The profit motive dictates major political decisions, and financial interest overrules human interest. The poor and powerless in the inner city are often manipulated by various welfare programmes, designed to perpetuate dependency and hopelessness. Also, there are so-called urban renewal schemes which some astute observers have rightly called 'poor people removal programmes.' Among the latest manipulation scheme by the powerful suburbanites is the regentrification movement.

Notice the arrogance of the term *regentrification* – the repopulation of the city. The use of the term suggests that those who never left the city – the poor, the minorities, the powerless – are non-persons. Are not the present inhabitants of the city, people? Are only those of Anglo-Saxon or European ethnicity considered people? It is ironic that many who were responsible for dissecting the city with motorways to facilitate their escape to suburbia are now returning. The victorious escape from ethnic minorities and the poor was a pyrrhic victory. In simple terms, the two or three hours per day in bumper-to-bumper traffic, burning expensive petrol, made the city seem a desirable habitat again.

Having discussed the sins of the powerless in the city as self-destruction and the sins of the powerful as self-deification and oppression, I ask, 'Is there a word from the Lord for the city?' There is a word for the church in the city.

A word of judgment: in Galatians 6:7 we read, 'Do not be deceived; God cannot be mocked. A man reaps what he sows.'

A word of instruction: in 1 Timothy 2:1–4 we read, 'I urge, then, first of all, that requests, prayers, intercession and thanksgiving be made for everyone – for kings and all those in authority, that we may live peaceful and quiet lives in all godliness and holiness. For this is good, and pleases God our Saviour, who wants all men to be saved and to come to a knowledge of the truth.'

A word of hope: in John 12:32 we read, 'But I, when I am lifted up from the earth, will draw all men to myself'.

Ministry in the city

Since God has not forsaken the city, the church must maintain a dynamic, compassionate servant ministry there. While the church holds to eternal and unchanging principles and truths, the application of the principles and methods of interpreting truth must have existential meaning. The church must maintain and preserve all that it can of its past liturgy, its worship, its teaching and healing ministry. Yet it must not be afraid of using new forms, methods and categories to proclaim the good news that God was in Christ, that the kingdom of God is come in Jesus of Nazareth, that Christ is Lord and he is Emmanuel – God with us – to show us all a better way.

Now the call to ministry in the city, like every call of God to ministry, is initially a call to prepare for service. The suffering servant must be 'thoroughly equipped for every good work' (2 Tim. 3:17). The equipping of the servant must follow a baptism of love which will enable the servant to represent Christ in a multi-cultural, multi-ethnic, multi-religious environment. This baptism of love will prepare the servant to remain faithful in the face of violence, hostility and other Satanic forces. The inner city provides an excellent opportunity for the Christian soldier to gain wounds for the cause of Christ. Here is an opportunity to get to know Christ in the fellowship of his suffering and to imitate Christ as a wounded healer.

At St Stephen Church of God in Christ, where I have been the founding pastor since 1962, we have seen the good hand of God prosper a work in the inner city. The congregation was organized with seven people in south-east San Diego, an area in transition. White flight had resulted in a leadership vacuum. In an area with approximately ninety thousand citizens, there was an influx of minorities, primarily Afro-Americans and Mexican-Americans. These newcomers were generally poor, unemployed or underemployed with limited skills and education. As an eyewitness to the community transition that took place during the decade from 1959–69, I observed that not only did the established churches abandon the area, but so did major grocery chains, some doctors and health-care professionals.

St Stephen responded to the needs of the neighbourhood in transition and began to develop a ministry to the whole person. This ministry has three broad emphases: (1) preaching, the proclaiming of the Word of God; (2) teaching, the

36

explaining and application of God's truth to the human situation; and (3) healing, the work of the Holy Spirit in the life of the believer and community of faith. Hereby the Word becomes flesh and 'dwells in the ghetto' for healing and reconciliation.

The central focus of our ministry is to win the lost to Christ, nurture the faithful and make disciples. We have worship in the church on a daily basis and Holy Communion on Fridays. We also conduct worship services 'on location' for shut-ins and sponsor small groups for nurture and Bible study.

We have educational programmes including a traditional Sunday school plus a Christian school – primary and secondary with college courses added in co-operation with local colleges. Family life must be emphasized in ministry in the city, for there the family breakdown is devastating. So we have couples conferences, singles conferences and other meetings for those who are engaged and those who are married. And we have seminars and workshops and drama activities, family camps, vacation Bible schools and summer camps. All of these tend to strengthen the fabric of the family in the inner city.

Special ministries are necessary for army camps, prisons, secondary schools, primary schools, colleges and universities.

There are, as well, street ministries to those who are completely down and out. Every Friday night when the action is going, thirty or forty of our young people go out in teams of twos to the red-light district and the bars and places where flesh is being peddled. Just their presence is a significant witness to God's love because many of them have come from that situation and they are going back. It is not uncommon for gangsters to bring in their drugs – heroin and the needles and the spoons – on a Sunday or during the week. One Sunday we were frightened to death when somebody brought his sawn-off shotgun to church, turning it in because he didn't need it anymore. The gospel is reaching those in the city.

We also provide emergency food and housing and counselling for families, drug abusers and alcoholics. We have job referral services and we train people for lay ministry in the city. We even have an outreach into Mexico and are helping to plant churches there.

Finally, we run a bookshop and a couple of half-way houses for rehabilitation. Then we also have the usual youth and family activities.

Indeed, God is not abandoning the city. In spite of moral and spiritual decay and socio-economic deterioration, in spite of every prophet of doom's statement that the city's sickness is unto death, the church must believe that even if there is spiritual, moral and economic death in the city, our God is able to speak life into it and call for resurrection in the city.

A spiritually dead and doomed Nineveh received God's word through Jonah, repented and lived. A desolate, disunited, despairing remnant in Jerusalem heard God's word through Nehemiah, and the walls and the gates were restored, and the city of Jerusalem came alive again. The Sanballats, Tobiahs and Geshems couldn't stop the movement of God. In more recent times, England was thrown into a deep spiritual darkness. Sin was rampant and the church to a great extent had become God's frozen people. But God's word came through John and

Charles Wesley until millions of hearts were strangely warmed and revival fires were ignited in the cities and hamlets throughout England. The course of history and the life of a nation were changed.

The destiny of our nation is inextricably bound to the destiny of our cities. God hears the cries and the hurting of the hopeless in the city. He sees the growing tensions between the powerful and the powerless, the haves and the have-nots. He knows the sin and the uncleanness that prevails there. The only power to save the city is God's redemptive power. And he uses human instruments.

God has asked a simple question. Who will go for us? Jesus gave a commission. In Acts 1:8 he has directed and commanded that we shall be his witness in the city of Jerusalem. We must go to Jerusalem, that great city that is explosive with religious bigotry and sectarianism. Jesus says go back to that city and preach the gospel of reconciliation, restoration, deliverance and healing, the gospel of power and hope. Go to Samaria with its riots and racial strife, with its slums and ghettos, with its immorality and sins, its poverty and filth. Go into the byways and the hedges and tell them that the good master has prepared a supper and has invited the poor and the disinherited and the halt and the blind to come to be blessed.

Finally, Christ has told us to go to the uttermost parts of the earth. Let neither sea nor mountain, language nor custom, colour nor race, suffering nor sacrifice hinder you. Don't let 'nobody' turn you around. Take the message of Christ everywhere.

George McKinney is pastor of St Stephen's Church of God in Christ, a large urban church in San Diego, California. He has written several books and pamphlets including, Pastoral Counselor Handbook, The Christian Home *and* Christian Marriage.

3
OVERCOMING THE REAL BARRIERS

RAY BAKKE

The call to missions is a personal one. But God does not give us mere advice, which we paternalistically deliver to the city, but news, news that liberates and sets people free from bondage. The fundamental difference is precisely this. Advice requires you to do something to make things work. News declares what God has already done for you in Jesus Christ. We go forth as persons called by a risen Christ to announce good news.

The lucid Sri Lanka expositor Ajith Fernando reminds us at the end of the book that God himself is a missionary. God is striving to enlarge our message and get his messengers to enlarge their maps. The mission of Jonah was to go to a city that was filled with hatred and war. The message of Jonah confronts the narcissism of the West, and it confronts the ethnocentric gospels which we wrap in flags and deliver to nations around the world.

World-class barriers

My task is to enlarge your map. I want to draw your attention to the shifting frontiers of mission today. I want to focus on a world that has gone from a world of nations to a world of interconnected multinational cities. It is a world of some 223 nations that is in reality a world of 300 world-class cities, a world growing so fast that by the year 2000 there will be nearly 500 cities of more than 1 million people. The barriers to mission and evangelism today are real and complex.

One of the barriers is simply the demographics. The United Nations has a department of 40 people that focuses on the demographics of cities. And the numbers are staggering. As you read this sentence a hundred babies will be born in the world. Forty-nine will be yellow. Thirteen will be white like me. The rest will be black and brown. Most of them will live in the cities of the world.

The monthly net growth of the world is more than the population of a city the size of metropolitan Chicago, with its 7.1 million people. There have not been a billion minutes since Jesus walked on this earth over nineteen hundred years ago, but we are going to produce a billion-and-a half new babies in the next thirteen or fourteen years. And without a doubt most of them will live in the cities.

For two thousand years we have had the Great Commission to go into all the world to preach the gospel to all peoples and make disciples of the nations. Now we know where they are – in my neighbourhood, in the cities, in London, in Frankfurt and the teeming cities around the world. The numbers are staggering – but so is the kaleidoscopic complexity of the cities. The city is like an escalator moving in the wrong direction – like a gigantic magnet sucking people from the jungles, from islands, from tribal groups.

For centuries western Europe could organize its life, its ideology, its world view around the Mediterranean. If you read Henri Pirenne's classic *Medieval Cities,* you will discover that Europe swung for 800 years like a slowly swinging door. She was pushed by Islam and pulled by the northern cities of Germany. Europe was forced to be a nation looking north and west. We have been in an Atlantic-perimeter world for the last 500 to 600 years. But now within this century, your lifetime and mine, the world is swinging again. The door is opening, only this time much faster, and we're shifting from an Atlantic to a Pacific-perimeter world. This new world is beckoning us with explosive and complex cities.

The fastest growing cities in the world are in Latin America, Africa and Asia, and they are changing the way we think, live and construct our economies. Sadly, the fastest growing cities are often in areas where the church is the weakest – in the Asian perimeter. So that scale of urban mission is measured not only by the size and number of the cities, but also by their changing configuration and complexity.

Mexico City, for example, is the oldest city in this hemisphere, but it is also the youngest. Twenty million people live in that city – try to imagine it – twenty times a million people. But while the median age in Chicago is 31, the median age in Mexico City is 14. That means there are some ten million people in Mexico City under 14 years of age. It is an old city and a young city.

Not long ago I was walking the streets of Toronto with a former student of mine, now a missionary there. We were looking at some of its 20,000 teenagers, and wanted to weep. Even more recently I was in Hollywood, observing some of the 5,000 teenagers on the streets of that city, selling their bodies. They have come from all over America drawn by a dream, but living on the streets.

Recently I heard the Ecumenical Night Ministry in Chicago tell the story of 10,000 teenagers on the Chicago streets. They are a city within a city. Thirty per cent of them are psychiatric mental cases, patients who were released from mental institutions and psychiatric hospitals when they lost funding.

The complexity of the city is that it isn't one city. It's a commercial city, an industrial city, a nocturnal city, a daytime city, an ethnic city, an international city, a migrant city, a student city, a five-star hotel city, a derelict city, a deviant city, an institutionalized city. People in cities are being packaged. To reach them is to deal with numbers, growth and complexity.

But many of these cities are not easily accessible to us. Thirty of the cities with populations of more than one million are in China. At least twenty of them are in the Soviet Union. Many of the fastest-growing cities in the world are in the Islamic world. Some are like Beirut, which may be a parable of the city. Today we know it as a violent city. But it is not well known that a decade ago, when the civil war began in Beirut, the population was one million. Today, after years of war and a multitude of deaths, the population of Beirut is about 1.8 million. In other words, the very pain and struggle of Beirut have served as a magnet to draw people out of south Lebanon into that city – and it's almost impossible for us to go in and do anything about that.

In 1980 the Lausanne Committee for World Evangelization held a conference in Thailand. My assignment was to help organize the urban part of that consultation. In the preparation we carried on correspondence with people in over a hundred cities. So I carried with me about 5,000 pages of primary research to that conference. We sat down with 110 people who were from six continents and began to look at what God was doing in the cities. We were amazed to find how little was being done by evangelicals and how few mission agencies seemed concerned about preparing missionaries for urban mission. We were also stunned by how God was using new means, new forms and new wineskins.

After that conference I was assigned to travel to about a hundred cities, holding consultations with people, taking a fresh look at their city and ministries on the one hand, and then asking, What are the new models of ministry that are needed to reach this city – whether it be Cairo, Copenhagen, Zagreb or Mexico City?

I had been taught in seminary by the late Paul Little that if people don't come to Christ or won't witness for him, it is because they lack two things – either information or motivation. But there is a third factor in urban mission: *intimidation*, the we-never-did-it-that-way-before syndrome. Those are the seven last words of the church.

Personal barriers

When we talk about urban mission today, clearly we are facing some very definite barriers. But three barriers confront you personally, and it seems to me that these personal ones are the real barriers: the theological, the ecclesiastical and the fear barriers.

The theological barrier. One of the internal barriers in the big, bad city is a theological one. Most of us have a personal theology, a personal conversion. I would call it a Philippian theology – a theology of Christ who left the heavens and came down to live within us. We have a 'my God and I' relationship – and it's wonderful. Most of us lack, however, a Colossian theology of a transcendent Christ, who is Lord of the systems and structures of the world, including those gigantic macro-structures of the metroplace, the city. And without that Colossian perspective, we have relief theology, but no theology of reform. We deal with victims, but we can't deal with the issues of justice.

A thief-on-the-cross theology – just enough to make it to heaven – is a place to start. But if we are to engage in urban mission, we are going to have to keep studying. In the words of Walter Scott, 'For a Christian one book is enough, but a thousand aren't too many.' It is a fact that with the Bible School training which I have, I could be the most educated person in many a village, but in many cases the city will not yield to minimalist education. Some of you will need to go on and study hard to apply that

Colossian theology. To personal theology you need to add a public theology of mission. We need not only a missiology of the city, but a biblical theology of the city.

To think biblically means to understand how God has moved in creation and redemption throughout biblical history. To think historically is to understand that the same Spirit of God that moves us today has also led God's people across cultures for the past two thousand years. We need these lessons from history because the city is a museum of art and architecture, a museum of cultures and peoples who come from the far corners of the globe and are being reshaped by the forces of the city.

Our need is to develop a world view that helps us see that the world now lives in my neighbourhood. There are sixty nations represented in my neighbourhood in Chicago, and in the state school where my kids went, lessons are taught in eleven languages. Thirty-five per cent of the neighbourhood is Black, but many distinct Black cultures are represented: tobacco culture, cotton culture, coal culture, Caribbean culture. Twenty-eight per cent are Asians, but they are all different. There are north, south and east Asians – some of them are refugees and poor, but many are a wealthy elite.

One of the real barriers to urban missions is the way we have read the Bible as a rural book. We sing 'Work for the Night Is Coming' and 'I Come to the Garden Alone' – hymns imbued with pastoral and rural imagery. But, as Bill Pannell says, it is very difficult for the urbanite in downtown Cleveland to think in terms of herding sheep. We need to expand our theology until it encompasses God's vision for the city.

The ecclesiastical barrier. Another major barrier is ecclesiastical. For many of us the church has been a club – my white, middle-class church could not survive when the neighbourhood changed. Many of us are the product of the white-flight, white-fright syndrome. We fled the city just when God brought the whole world there.

Some of us feel guilty about that. But let me tell you, when you left the city, the Spirit didn't leave. He just jumped into other wineskins. Today the fastest growing churches are often Black, Hispanic or Korean – and many of them worship in languages other than English. The Lord doesn't need you to come back to Chicago as a Messiah sent to save the city. If you come, you must join him in the work he is already doing there.

Today denominations and mission boards are struggling to understand how they should divide the turf. Whereas in the past they could distinguish between home mission and foreign mission, today those distinctions don't make much sense – what is home and what is foreign cannot be so easily distinguished. The Southern Baptist Home Mission ministers in twenty-six languages in Los Angeles alone. The archdiocese of Chicago must deal with twenty-two languages. The foreign field has come home.

Today we need to think in terms of mission to the *geographically* distant – that mission to reach a billion or more people living far from any existing church – and the new frontier of mission to the *culturally* distant – that two-and-a-half billion people who live within the shadows of existing churches. We will still need missionaries to cross oceans, mountains and deserts to reach unreached peoples. But the new frontier is in the cities constructed from the mass migrations and exploding birth rates of our day. This is the new reality of world mission.

One of the assignments I enjoy giving to classes on urban mission is to take them into a supermarket and give them thirty minutes to observe what is happening in the neighbourhood. They come out and tell me how the food business has changed in the last thirty, even fifteen years. Stores are open twenty-four hours a day. Everything has been computerized. Prices have gone up. While stores used to carry eight thousand products, they now stock twenty-four thousand. They have Asian, Spanish, Geritol, and salt-free sections. Other sections cater for microwave people. They have foreign-language check-out assistants, and their cheque-cashing service is more convenient than my bank. Gone are days when the meat-cutters union could say 'We will not sell meat after six o'clock.'

Then I take my students over to a nearby church, and we look at the sign. And what do we see? Morning worship: 11.00 a.m. – as it was in the beginning, is now and ever shall be, world without end.

My question is, How can a supermarket without the Spirit of God do what the church doesn't seem to be able to do with the Spirit? How can we liberate the church to reach the city? How can we persuade foreign missionary societies to team up with the home mission in teaching the cross-cultural skills we now need at home? How can we do that? For most of us this is a greater barrier even than Islam.

The fear barrier. The third barrier is intensely personal – it has to do with our fear of the city. My cousin Gordon went to Zambia, after we entered Moody Bible Institute together thirty-one years ago. He is a hero. He is a missionary, with pythons and cobras in his garden. I've got news for him: I've got Pythons and Cobras and Latin Kings in my back yard.

Many Christians who admire my cousin Gordon think I'm stupid to raise my family in the city. There is a dichotomy in the minds of many of us as we think about the city. Many of the great missionary heroes buried their children in foreign lands. But if you take your children to the city today, someone is going to tell you that you are abusing them. You are going to alienate them from the mainstream of our culture. I have heard this argument, and I reject it.

Jesus Christ is Lord of the city. We desperately need families in the city. We need children, for they quickly adapt to the culture and give us access to it. They give us reasons to be involved in the schools. We need Christians back in public housing projects, back in the labour unions, back in the playgrounds and grammar schools. We can't afford to pull them out.

We cannot fight the battle for the cities the way America fought the war in Vietnam. We parked our planes on Guam, flew them at 37,000 feet, bombed people to hell, went back for a night's sleep and lost the war. You cannot blitz the cities and expect to win the battle. We have to incarnate the gospel, wrap it up and deliver it in person to the street. The personal challenge is a barrier for many of us. Jonah found it a barrier.

Are you concerned enough to overcome the barriers? The statistics are staggering. Humanly and mathematically speaking, we are losing the battle for the city. (I say that apart from what the Spirit of God might do and how you might figure in those numbers.) The complexity of the city is overwhelming, and the stunning reality is that the bigger a city gets, the less we can comprehend and communicate that complexity. Social psychologists speak of this as the psychology of overload.

The sheer complexity of the city is staggering, not to speak of the Beiruts, the Sowetos and Nicosias that are locked behind restrictive national borders. But let me remind you of the three barriers you need to confront.

First, you need to overcome the theological barrier, that seven-foot hump between your personal faith and the faith that equips you for the full-orbed mission of the church in the world of today.

Second, you need to get over the ecclesiastical barrier that looks at the church as a little club and start asking hard questions about how we build churches within the complex structures and ethnicity of our cities. How can the church at home become the foreign church, and how can we speak with integrity about the global mission of the local church in a world in which the nations have come to live with us?

Finally, you need to confront the personal challenge. You will always be a minority in the city – racially, spiritually, ideologically, politically and almost every other way. Are you ready? Remember Romans 8:31: 'If God is for us, who can be against us?' Go for it, and God bless you.

Ray Bakke, author of The Urban Christian (MARC Europe, 1987), *lectures in ministry at Northern Baptist Theological Seminary and is senior and associate international co-ordinator for the Lausanne Committee for World Evangelization.*

4
THE STREETS OF AMSTERDAM

FLOYD McCLUNG, JR.

I have been living and working with my wife and our two children in the city of Amsterdam with Youth With A Mission for the last fourteen years. We live in the red-light district of Amsterdam, which is twelve blocks long and six blocks wide. There are sixteen thousand prostitutes who live and work in that neighbourhood and twelve thousand drug addicts. There are also six thousand male prostitutes. In fact, Amsterdam is one of the gay capitals of Europe.

When we moved into the red-light district, two doors to the right of us was a Satanist church. Four doors to the right of us was a homosexual brothel. And two doors to the left of us was a twenty-four hour porno cinema. We didn't write home about our neighbours very often.

The original purpose my wife Sally and I had in coming to Amsterdam was to work with alienated young people. We started a half-way house, but not long after we arrived, we became concerned for the entire city. One of the first things I did was to walk the streets to try to get a feel for the city, to get to know it, to get God's heartbeat for the city. I once heard Billy Graham say that if he ever started a ministry anywhere in a city, he would spend six months walking its streets getting to know the people and the neighbourhoods and praying. I took that advice literally.

As I began to walk the streets and to pray for the people, I became acquainted with the various neighbourhoods and people groups. It was an overwhelming and daunting experience. There was neighbourhood after neighbourhood of high-rise apartment buildings. The city of Amsterdam has about 2.5 million people in the metropolitan area and about eight hundred thousand in the city proper.

I tried to find all the evangelical churches I could in the city, but I discovered only seven or eight that preached the gospel. I went to the university campus. I went into the inner city. I went to places where young people hung out. I went to the ethnic neighbourhoods. I saw building after building, and home after home, person after person who did not know the Lord Jesus Christ, and it all semed to be too much for me. I felt that there was hardly any hope. Humanly speaking, it seemed impossible.

I remember one night in particular. I knelt and began to pray in desperation to the Lord. In fact, I gave the Lord an opportunity to admit that he had made a mistake in inviting me to come to the city.

But he didn't change his mind. Instead he began to call me to work alongside other Christians who were in the city. Together he wanted to use us to make an impact on that city. As I prayed, faith began to grow in my heart that God could make a difference.

I had been reading the book of Jonah, and I was struck by how weak Jonah was. He went in the opposite direction when God called him to Nineveh. He was a proud prophet, a man who hated the Assyrians, the arch-enemies of Israel. Yet that was the man God used in Nineveh. He went and simply proclaimed the gospel, and God used his obedience to make a profound impact on that city. The whole city turned toward God in fasting and prayer. And I began to believe that it could happen again. If God could touch the wicked city of Nineveh, the capital of Assyria, then he could touch the city of Amsterdam.

I took a little piece of paper out, as I knelt in prayer, and I began to list all of the peoples that I had seen as I walked the streets – the university students, the drug addicts, the homosexuals. I listed all of the minority and ethnic groups I could find. There are one hundred and fifteen languages spoken in the city of Amsterdam and forty-four major ethnic neighbourhoods. As I listed the people groups, I began to ask the Lord to somehow start a ministry among every one of those peoples. I prayed that they would experience God's grace and God's hope in a way that would be understandable and meaningful to them.

Not a Christian city – yet
That was fourteen years ago, and today I am thankful to tell you that God has begun to answer

55

those prayers. When we first went to Amsterdam, there was no association of Christian groups or ministers. In fact, I invited some of the Christian leaders to meet on the little houseboat where we lived. It was so unusual in the nation of Holland at that time for evangelical ministers and leaders to meet together that the national news media sent out a television crew to film it.

We began to meet monthly. That group has met every month since that time. We call it The Evangelical Contact. There are now more than fifty churches and parachurch organizations that meet every month and have a wonderful spirit of unity. God has begun to touch the city of Amsterdam.

We were thrilled when Billy Graham came with the International Congress for Itinerant Evangelists in 1983 and again in 1986. Can you imagine ten thousand evangelists sitting in a conference for two weeks without preaching? Impossible. Every street corner had a black or a brown or a yellow face proclaiming the gospel. Every tram and train and bus had moving street meetings.

During the conference my wife was walking down the street and heard a man mumbling to himself. As she walked beside him, he was shaking his head and mumbling the word Jesus.' 'Oh, Jesus, Jesus, Jesus,' he said. 'Everywhere I go I can hear nothing but Jesus.'

One young German tourist saw teams of young people with crosses. (Arthur Blessitt had been to town, so we had crosses everywhere.) Innocently she asked one of our workers, 'I've gone to almost every major square in the city. I've been in bars and cafes and restaurants. Everywhere I've gone I've met

Christians. Is this a Christian city?' It's not a Christian city – yet.

A week of ministry

In our organization, Youth With A Mission, there are over two hundred staff working full-time in the city. There are twenty-four full-time evangelistic and caring ministries. We have church planting teams, halfway houses, neighbourhood Bible studies and a church renewal team. There are children's Bible clubs, bands, drama groups, a ministry to prostitutes and urban training programmes.

I'd like to take you through a week so you can see what God has done. On Tuesday night there is a Bible study that is led by my former secretary. Laura was a missionary in South America for about sixteen years. She's sixty-nine years old. Four years ago she said to me, 'I would like to start a Bible study for Spanish-speaking prostitutes.' Thousands of them in the city have been brought in from Latin America. So she started with two or three people four years ago. Today she has Bible studies for seventy converted Spanish-speaking prostitutes on three nights of the week in three different cities. The result? I've lost my secretary. A few weeks ago she told me, 'I can't serve you and keep going with the Bible studies. They are multiplying too much. You'll have to find another secretary.'

Also on Tuesday night we have a work in the red-light district that is centred in what we call The Cleft. The Cleft is a little residence, a retreat, a hiding place for people in need who come to us. We also run a restaurant, where we serve Dutch pancakes. One Christmas, a Muslim man joined us for some free meals during the holidays. He had experienced the fellowship and the warmth. He went back to Germany where he lived and didn't quite understand how to contact us, so he wrote a letter and addressed it to The Cleft Pancake House Church.

Every Tuesday night, workers from The Cleft go on the streets of the red-light district and invite prostitutes, drug addicts and anybody who will come to a Bible study. They share the gospel, they give a free meal, and more than that they get involved in people's lives. For example, a few weeks ago there was a lady I'll call Paula who was standing out in front of The Cleft. She was invited in for a meal. After a lot of imploring she finally came. Paula had been a prostitute and a heroin addict for over twenty years. That night the grace of God finally broke into Paula's life. Weeping, she discovered that God loved her and forgave her.

Paula is now in a rehabilitation programme. Every time I've seen her in the last few months, there has been a glow on her face. She can hardly enter into a Bible study or a Christian church service without weeping because of the joy that she has found in being forgiven by the Lord Jesus.

On Wednesday nights we have a Bible study that is for punks and other Amsterdam young people. About three years ago, a young man on our staff named David said he was concerned for the alienated youth of Amsterdam, especially the punkers. It is estimated that one out of every three seventeen-year-olds in Amsterdam is involved in homosexuality. Seventy per cent of the children born in the inner city are born to unwed mothers. Because of the surveys we have done, we estimate that in the nation of Holland eighty-five to ninety per cent of the young people are still interested in God, but they have turned their backs on formal religion. It is a city with tremendous social problems and tremendous spiritual potential for the young.

For eighteen months David and his team of workers went out night after night into the nightclubs and the cafes of the city. They did not see one person respond to the gospel.

Then about a year and a half ago, they started a Bible study. Young people began to come. David is very contemporary (and very appropriate to Amsterdam) in the way he communicates. He started a punk band called No Longer Music. Some would debate whether it's a band or not. They do make noise. Joyful noise. It's a very colourful Bible study they have now. It's been a breakthrough. About one hundred and fifty punks have come to know the Lord Jesus along with many other Amsterdam young people.

Eddie, one of the young people who became a Christian, was kicked out of his home when he was eight years old. His father told him he never wanted to see Eddie again. That was eleven years ago. A year ago, Eddie heard about what the press had begun to call the Chrunk movement – the Christian punks. (Leave it to the press to come up with a name like that.) As a result he came to David's Bible study. When Eddie saw young people like himself who were excited about God, who were dealing with the issues that he was facing, he considered Christianity.

Eddie found Jesus Christ a few weeks later, and then a national television team came and interviewed him. He gave his testimony. His father saw Eddie on television for the first time in ten years. The next day Eddie got a telephone call. The day after that they had lunch together, and they were reconciled together as father and son after ten years of alienation.

Also on Wednesday nights, a Christian family in another part of the city leads a new congregation. They moved into a neighbourhood of about twenty-five thousand people where there was no active church and began a Bible study. The husband began going door-to-door while still working in business full time. Later he brought in teams of people to help him. Now there is a new church in that neighbourhood.

On Thursday nights we have a Bible study for Iranians. There are many refugees from Iran all over Europe. There's a young man, a German, who leads our work with Muslims. On Friday nights he leads a Bible study for Moroccans. I asked Harry why he didn't have the Bible study on the same night since the Iranians and Moroccans were both Muslims. He reminded me that there was a war going on in the Middle East. He said, 'My goal is to get both groups converted and then we'll bring them together.'

On Saturday, believe it or not, we have a Bible study for normal people. We have a young lady who co-ordinates our follow-up in Amsterdam, and she came to me very excited in the spring of this year. 'Floyd, you won't believe this! We've had a great breakthrough. Yesterday in the outreach, two normal Dutch girls got saved.'

One of the young men who became a Christian in

60

our work when we first moved to Amsterdam fourteen years ago was John Goodfellow, a thief from the streets of Nottingham, England. After going back to Nottingham to make restitution for some of the crimes he committed, he rejoined us. He'd seen a street preacher in Nottingham, and he wanted to preach on the streets of Amsterdam.

At that time we emphasized friendship evangelism. I had experienced street meetings, but I didn't like them. I had seen people standing on street corners in America preaching about hell and yelling at people. I had a negative impression of what street meetings were like. So when John asked about this, I said, 'No way!' And a few weeks later, he came and asked me again. And I said, 'No, we're into friendship evangelism. We want to care for people. We love people. We don't want to yell at them.'

Over a six-month period, he came back to me about every two or three weeks. He wouldn't give up. One night, I was walking down the hallway in the building where we were living, and I heard a voice. Listening more closely, I realized someone was praying. It was John, weeping and crying as he interceded with God. Then I heard him praying for me, 'Oh, God, please change his mind. Lord, touch his heart. Please, Lord, let him give me permission to go on the streets and preach the gospel.'

So the next day I said to John that he could go – on two conditions. 'John, please don't yell at people, and please don't talk about hell.' He was so excited he would have done anything. John with some others went out on the streets of Amsterdam to the main square, and I stood in the back of the crowd and watched. They used some folk dancing to attract a crowd. Dutch people, especially the Amsterdamers as we call them, love something that has joy, that has humour in it.

John told the people about the joy the Lord had brought into his heart as somebody who had found Jesus on the streets of Amsterdam. He shared how he had become a thief, running from the law, running from problems. But he had found the joy of his salvation in Jesus, I was amazed as I stood watching at how open people were to a loving, joyful presentation of the good news of the gospel. We outjoyed the joy that they had known in the world. Many people came to those meetings that we began to conduct on the streets.

I began to read about the early days of the Salvation Army, and I read a book called *The General Next to God*. The Salvation Army was too stubborn to give up. When they went into a city, if they couldn't penetrate it, they tried something else. They would keep trying different approaches, with different people groups until finally they would break through.

I read about one young lady, an officer in the Salvation Army, who was having a hard time in one city. So she decided to have a funeral. She got a coffin, got a young officer to be the dead person and put him in the coffin. They walked down the street and finally stopped and leaned the coffin against the building. When the crowd they gathered was big enough, this young man jumped out and began to preach on 'The wages of sin is death.'

So I told John about this, and a few days later heard some hammering in our basement. I went downstairs and discovered John building a seven-foot black coffin. Since that time we've had many funeral services in Amsterdam.

John now heads a ministry in Amsterdam we call the Go Teams. This last summer, between May and August, John had teams in nineteen different countries. A team in Bombay helped to plant five churches in three months working with missionaries there. Another team was in North Africa working with a small, struggling church of about sixty believers. It was doubled in two and a half weeks as seventy people found faith in Jesus Christ. They're still preaching the gospel.

The dark continent

I love the city of Amsterdam. I celebrate the Lord Jesus in that city. I believe that God longs for and looks for those who will go to the cities of our world. Amsterdam is a city that is surrounded within a mile radius by one hundred and fifty million people. Europe is a continent of great need, a spiritual wasteland.

Though there is great revival in China, though the church is growing three times as fast as the population in Latin America, though there are some days in Africa that up to twenty thousand people a day become Christians, in Europe we have not yet experienced the touch of God's Spirit in great renewal. We have not seen the church turned around. There are five hundred and fifty million people living in Western Europe. About seventy per cent of them live in cities, and of that seventy per cent, it is estimated that less than two per cent go to church on Sundays.

I present to you Europe as a mission field.

I remind you of cities like Amsterdam and Paris and London which desperately need the gospel of Jesus Christ. Amsterdam has more than four hundred financial institutions. It's one of the seven or eight most influential financial cities in the world. It is a city that waits to hear the good news of Jesus Christ.

I discovered in reading the book of Jonah that God uses ordinary people to do extraordinary things. If we will simply follow the example of our Lord Jesus, if we will give up our rights, if we will be willing to give up our reputation, if we will come as servants to stand beside people, not over them but beside them, to love them and share joyfully and lovingly and patiently the good news that we have discovered, many people will respond.

Floyd McClung is executive director of international operations and director of urban missions for Youth With A Mission, a worldwide ministry training young adults in missions.

5
THE INVISIBLE PEOPLE
HARVIE M. CONN

What is a city? For a western white, a city is a melting pot. For a suburbanite it's a ghetto. For my next-door neighbour in inner-city Philadelphia, a city is 'one large collection of nothings.'

Now all these definitions are wrong, and they're all wrong for the same reason. Yuppie, suburbanite or black, most people can't see anything in the city except mathematical urban units of one. They're often like the pastor I met once as a missionary in Korea. At a moment of truth he confided in me, 'I have a very hard time telling all you Americans apart. You look so alike.' I think that's how we all see cities. They all look so alike – a sort of an urbanized Charles Bronson death wish.

A rose is a rose is a rose. And a city is a city is a city – a monoclass stereotype where everything becomes the least pleasant denominator. And when you see nothing else, you resort again to that Norman Rockwell world view, the melting-pot myth where everything looks so nice and everyone is equal – of course some are more equal than others. In this scheme we're all in this together, and there's plenty of room for those that must sit in the back of the bus. We're all one big happy family. Tell that to the single parent on welfare in Newark, New Jersey. Ethnic differences, poor and rich neighbourhoods, Yuppies, blue-collar workers, physicians, roofers – they all slowly evaporate into this new homogeneity that is usually identified only as urban.

Now, what does all this have to do with world missions? The fact is that you can't reach what you can't see.

Take a look, for example, at Lima, Peru. If you took your first look in 1984, you would find a city somewhere between four and a half and six million people, which, by the way, accounts for one-third of the total population of Peru. In 1982 people were moving into the capital city of Lima at a rate of 230 people per day. Today it is several times that figure, but if that is all you notice about Lima, your picture is still too general. You still haven't seen what you need to see to minister effectively there.

Lima is full of migrants, migrants from the provinces and the remotest Andean villages. And as you look closely, you will notice that they don't lose their identity as soon as they get off the bus. You won't see them with their knees shaking, looking around ready to have a mental breakdown because suddenly they've made it to the big city. Instead they come to the city and form social clubs, organized around their home locality. These regional clubs give them a place to gather, to feel at home in their new surroundings, a buffer zone that cushions the impact of the new urban world that they are part of. In 1957 there were 200 such associations in Lima. By 1984 there were more than 6,000. Now don't tell these people that Lima is a melting pot. Lima is a salad bowl. In fact, it may be 6,000 salad bowls awaiting the gospel's salad dressing.

Look again. Here's another Lima – the Lima you see on the street, an army of street venders, 200,000 to 300,000 strong. Up to seventy per cent of the urban labour force in Lima make up this non-formal business world.

Look again and see Lima's 10,000 abandoned children. They shine shoes, wash cars, change tires and go begging during the day. At night they sleep in parks or on the sidewalk. They are a part of the fifty per cent of Lima's population that is under 22 years of age.

When you look at Lima like this, what do you see? You see magnetic centres that are sucking or pulling people into their fields. These magnetic fields are people groups. And they pull in different ways. Sometimes the pull is language or ethnicity. For example, 30% of the 18,000,000 Peruvians speak only Quechua. Yet there are only two Quechua-language evangelical congregations in all of Lima.

Sometimes the bonding that holds people together is geography, social space, a commonly shared residential territory. Migrants, for example, in Lima pour into something called the *pueblos jóvenes*, a euphemism meaning 'young towns' to the government, but 'slums' to the city. Three out of every ten Limeños live in one of these young towns. The children who fill them live on a cup of tea and a couple of bread rolls a day. And an inflation rate of 125% keeps them there.

Sometimes the bonding that brings people together into a group is non-geographic social space. The street vendors and abandoned children represent such groups. Sometimes vocations bring non-neighbours together. Sometimes it's common interests.

For seven years in Korea I did evangelistic work in brothels, sharing Christ with the country's prostitute population of over 50,000. They too represent a people group. A new and massive people group has emerged in just the last decade. It crosses ethnic, linguistic and even social barriers. I speak of those suffering from AIDS.

Some months ago I was visiting the midwest, and a friend invited me to go to a midnight prayer meeting. We went into a terraced house and up a set of rickety stairs and opened the door. There was a long table and about twelve people sitting around it, all with Bibles in front of them with beer cans strewn all over the smoke-filled room.

The Bible study leader was at the end, smoking a long, black cigar – and she really enjoyed it. At the other end of the table was a guy, built like Sylvester Stallone, wearing a black T-shirt with a white skull on it. On one arm was a big tattoo, a heart with the word *mother* on it and a big dagger through it.

So we sat down for a two-hour Bible study. Having been teaching at a typical white suburban

68

theological seminary where everything's safe, I had my doubts when things started, but when we were done, I had no doubts about what was going on. These were people who really loved the Lord, most of them brand new believers. The gentleman at the end of the table with the tattoo had been responsible for leading almost everyone there to Christ.

These were bikers. They wouldn't feel much at home in our community or in most of our churches. Two or three of the members of the Bible study were former members of Hell's Angels. A member of the Christian Biker's Association, the fellow who started the Bible study spends six months of the year with his wife on the road, and his whole ministry is spent trying to reach bikers for Jesus. 'Most outsiders,' he told me, 'are turned off by the beer and cigars. You ought to have seen what they were smoking and drinking a few months ago. Some Christians start at 1; others, at −3.'

I had found another unreached people group, one I didn't have to travel overseas to find. And I had also been reminded that sanctification follows justification, not vice versa.

What does this all mean for world evangelization? It means we need to realize that cities are not single, homogeneous little packages – Limas, Lisbons and Los Angeleses. They are conglomerates of thousands of different people groups. There are TV-movie entertainers in Seoul, soccer teams playing in São Paulo, Brazil; there are truck drivers spending 12–15 hours on the road between Osaka and Tokyo. There are the cosmopolitans of Singapore, who communicate only in English, their class-consciousness high, their ethnic-consciousness low.

Last summer, as a classroom experiment, I sent three teams of missionaries to Times Square in New York. Their assignment: to survey the same area of about six city blocks in the course of an evening and to come back the next day with a list of fifteen unreached peoples.

The next morning we all gathered to present our lists. They included over fifty people groups with an overlap of only three or four. In the same area we came across only three Christian groups and churches, and only one of those, we found out, was working with the people in that area. We also found that the bars in the area were much more aware of people groups than the church. There were gay bars, singles bars, bars for the theatre crowd and bars for newspaper people. Remember the opening line of the Cheers theme song, '... where everybody knows your name'?

We had begun to see the unreached people of the city, visible to God, but too often invisible to us. On our list we put prostitutes, sidewalk vendors, tourists, police, gays, theatre people, teenage runaways, bag ladies, the homeless, store owners. We found all sorts of gospel targets and no sharpshooters. And we were also discovering that if you aim at everything, you will hit nothing.

Urban people groups from the New Testament

Look with me at still another city with its people groups. We'll pick one with heavy population density, perhaps 200 people per acre, the equivalent of the industrial slums of Chicago or Philadelphia. This city has been devastated by war, and it has been rebuilt and gentrified by its Yuppie population.

It has become a thriving commercial centre and capital of its province. Its reputation is built on a combination of religion and sex – all without benefit of television or industrial-strength mascara. It's name has become a proverb for the good life, for a free-wheeling lifestyle. We're talking, of course, about the city of Corinth in the days of the apostle Paul.

The Lord had told the apostle Paul on his first visit to Cornith not to be afraid. 'You don't have to hide in the suburbs, man. Don't forget what I did for Moses in Egypt. There are a lot of good folks in the city.' That's my rough paraphrase of Acts 18:10.

Now when you read Romans, probably written from Corinth, and Paul's two letters written to the Christians in Corinth, you can see how God kept his promise. High and low, rich and poor, Jew and Greek – all the social, political and ethnic networks are there, and the gospel is touching them all.

Erastus – you find his name in the last chapter of Romans – either the director of the public works department (NIV) or the city treasurer (RSV) is there in Corinth. The aristocracy is being touched as well as the influential and the wealthy. 1 Corinthians 1 mentions Crispus. He came to Christ during Paul's first visit. Acts 18:8 calls him a ruler of the synagogue. That was a leader of the Jewish worship service, someone who assumed responsibility for the synagogue building. It also meant a man with money, social influence, far beyond the boundaries of the Jewish community itself.[1] I wonder if that isn't why in Acts 18:8 we read of the great impact of Crispus's conversion on the city. '. . . many of the Corinthians who heard him believed and were baptised.'

He had a baptismal partner named Gaius. Romans 16:23 informs us that he was 'host of the whole church' at Corinth, and that certainly means that he had a house big enough to put up Paul and to accommodate all the various Christian groups in Corinth that met together. He too was a fellow with some wealth and property.

At the other end of the social scale were the slaves, and the Corinthian Christian community included them as well. In fact, the numerical strength of the Corinthian church probably heavily leaned towards the have-nots of society. That's how God builds his church. With the wise and the powerful and the have-nots, all together doing the work of Jesus Christ.

In 1 Corinthians 1:26–28 Paul draws some gospel lessons against the background of these social realities. He paints a sociological picture of the church. There are 'the wise,' the educated classes; there are 'the influential'; there are those of 'noble birth.' But there are 'not many' of these in the church, though there are some.

By contrast, there are 'the lower born,' 'the despised,' 'the things that are not.' Primarily, among these people groups, 'the refuse of the world, the offscouring of all things' (1 Cor. 4:10–13 RSV), the church grows. And, says Paul in his best theological voice, that is the usual way God does things.

Is it easy to build an urban church out of such diverse groups? Not if Paul's experience is typical. A good sample of the problems is given in 1 Corinthians chapter 1.

Ethnic differences pick away at the gospel. Greeks look for wisdom; Jews look for power. What is needed is a new vision of Christ crucified, 'the power of God and the wisdom of God' (1 Cor. 1:24). Social differences create conceit. Wealthy and influential Christians presumably were looking down their 'noble born' noses at the 'have not' Christians. The answer, says Paul, is God's weird peculiarities of grace in election, the foolish things of this world chosen to shame the wise (1 Cor. 1:27–28).

Biblical guidelines for creating the unreached in the city

What do we learn when we read and hear all of this? There are at least three messages from Paul's picture of Corinth to us. Pull them out of your postbag.

1. The cutting edge of the church in the city is evangelism. The cities of Paul's day were crowded with voluntary associations and private clubs. Mainly they existed for the purpose of getting together, especially for people of like interests and occupations. They had regular meetings, their odd-ball Shriner-like initiation rites and special meals.[2]

The Christian church looked a lot like one of these special clubs, I suspect. That's how they survived at first in the city. They had their regular meetings, they had their initiation rites, they looked a little kooky, they had their special meals, but they were a different kind of club. They were the only club that existed for the sake of its non-members. Always before our eyes, says Paul in his letters, must be those on the outside.

Artisans, says Paul, are to lead a quiet life, to mind their own business and to work with their hands (1 Thes. 4:11). Why? That their 'daily life may win the respect of outsiders' (1 Thes. 4:12). Likewise, the Corinthian Christians must put no stumbling block before Jews and Greeks. The exercise of the gift of tongues in public assembly is to be restrained if visiting unbelievers get the wrong idea and think we Christians are insane. Any practices judged as disgraceful by the Gentiles must be curtailed (1 Cor. 11:4–6). Colossians 4:5 sums it up: 'Be wise in the way you act towards outsiders; make the most of every opportunity.'

Evelyn Quema, a short, stout, single Filipina, is barely noticeable in a crowd of women her age. At the age of 22 she gave up her desire to be a lawyer or a doctor and moved to the city of Baguio. She arrived on a Thursday with six dollars and no place to live. By Sunday she had conducted a church service for thirty and saw four conversions. Three years later she had planted four churches and started eleven outstations, one of them five hours away by bus. She had seen 300 solid conversions to Christ and several hundred more professions that she had not been able to follow up. Miriam Adeney, who tells this story, adds. 'There are hundreds of Christian women like Evelyn in southeast Asia.'

2. *The cutting edge of the church in the city is evangelism to all unreached peoples.* Paul's churches saw that. Membership went from slave owner to slave (Eph. 6:5–9; Col. 3:22–4:1), from the household of Caesar to manual labourers, skilled or unskilled (Phil. 4:22; 2 Thes. 3:6–13). We find wealthy artisans and traders like Lydia with high incomes but low occupational prestige. We find poor Christians in Jerusalem, recipients of financial support from poor Christians in Corinth and Macedonia (1 Cor. 16:1–4).

74

This is one of the reasons that the poor are so prominent in the New Testament. It is not because they have special privileges in heaven or because they can get in on the basis of an empty savings account. Rather, it is because God really does love every economic and social class, and because the wealthy, and sadly enough even wealthy Christians, are often in danger of forgetting them. Marginalized minorities and powerful majorities – the Lord has room for all of them in his church.

There are about 10,000 Muslims in my city, Philadelphia. About 80% of them are American Blacks. Too many of them are like my former next-door neighbour. They grew up in Christian homes, worshipped in Christian churches and finally turned to Islam. Why? My neighbour put it to me this way, 'The most segregated hour of the week in America is Sunday morning at 11:00 a.m. I dig Jesus. I just don't like his church.' An unreached people have become an invisible people.

The picture is the same around the world. The church in too many cities listen to too many sermons on success rather than suffering, while many feel left out in the ecclesiastical cold.

The industrial workers of Taiwan – three million of them – complain 'that the message of local churches is irrelevant to their daily life and most programmes are geared toward the needs of the intellectuals or the middle class.'[3] Over 40% of Singapore's workforce is blue collar, production-industry workers. Yet only 4% of them are Christians.

At the bottom of society's value scale, and often the church's, are the poor, the squatters, the new urban migrants. Forty-six per cent of Mexico City's population, 67% of Calcutta's, 60% of Kinshasa's, live in slums. And the gap between them and the church now grows into a gulf.

Yet they hear the word gladly. A missionary recounted to me how he had targeted Japanese businessmen for Christ, inviting them to play golf with him. Their response to this 'golf evangelism' was largely negative, but one of the caddies listened as they walked and talked. He in turn talked to other caddies, many of whom came to Christ through his witness. This missionary was wise enough to see what the Holy Spirit was doing and shifted his attention to a people group he had never seen before – Japanese golf caddies.

How do you tell which unreached people group in the city to focus on when there are so many? You watch for the footprints of the Lord and follow that trail.

Viv Grigg, a New Zealander, has made the same discovery about Jesus, 'a companion to the poor.' In 1979 he moved into Tatalon, a squatter community of 14,500 people, jammed into six city blocks in Manila. Now he pleads for the Lord's people to join him in creating Christian communities in the slums and shanty towns of the world. A new mission board has come out of his kingdom perspective called Servants among the Poor. An old vision has been renewed: mobile men and women, freed for pioneering, prophetic, evangelistic church planting among the poor. How does he put it? 'The greatest mission surge in history has entirely missed the greatest migration in history, the migration of Third World peasants to great mega-cities.'[4]

3. The cutting edge of the church in the city is lordship evangelism – Jesus proclaimed by word and deed, Jesus our justification and our justice.

A biblical call to repentance and faith in Christ does not call us away from the city; it calls us to live under the Lordship of Jesus Christ in every area of the city. Personal commitment to Jesus is foundational. But on that foundation we erect a model home, living out the full implications of the gospel for urban Christians.

Isn't that how Paul saw it as he wrote to Corinth? I have heard people say that Paul never dealt with social, political or economic issues. But that doesn't square with the list of pastoral questions he tries to answer in 1 Corinthians – ethnocentrism, the social gap between rich and poor, lawsuits, sex and prostitutes, slavery, homosexuality, women's liberation.

Cities like Corinth or Colombo don't let you get away with dividing your Christian life into safety zones – one zone labelled faith, another the world. Ask Malcolm X. American racism turned him from talkative Christianity to what he saw as real brotherhood in Islam. Ask the Black Christians of Soweto. A plea for peace without justice can turn good news into cheap grace. 'I was sick and you did not look after me; I was under the ban and you never visited me.' Ask the Blacks and Asians who come to missionary conferences. Ask them why you have to search so hard to find their brothers and sisters on the mission field abroad or on the platform or on the missionary society boards. It's hard to hear 'Go into all the world' when the same voices don't also say, 'Come into all our neighbourhoods.'

Paul saw a social revolution brewing in the things we now identify as 'church matters.' A simple table meal to remember the Lord's death shatters social hierarchies long held sacred. At Corinth the wealthy apparently were making the Lord's Supper into a 'private dinner party' (1 Cor. 11:21). And when the meal was over, the haves were drunk and the have-nots were hungry. Paul calls for a new kind of urban social order to be built from the table and the sacrifice that had prepared it (1 Cor. 10:16–17; 11:18–19). Wealth in the body of Christ becomes an opportunity to serve, prestige a call to humility.

None of this is easy in the city. Political and social networks fit together too tightly. You may find yourself one day a missionary pastor in a Central American country, the members of your congregation united in their commitment to Christ but divided in their political allegiances. Late one evening a knock may come to your door. There in front of you stands a member of your congregation, a brother in Christ with strong anti-government sympathies. There is a bullet in his arm; blood drips down his coat. 'Pastor,' he asks, 'can I stay the night with you?' Suddenly your Christian response to a brother becomes a political decision.

More than ten years ago I was on a mountain in Korea. I was up there for three days of evangelistic meetings at an isolated village with no electricity. I was talking that night on the love of Christ and how Christians love one another, and at the end asked if there were any questions. An old man raised his hand and said 'I have a question, sir,' he said. 'If Christians are supposed to love one another, how do you explain what happened in Birmingham?'

There we were on the top of the mountain in the middle of nowhere and this old farmer with a horsehair hat asked me about Birmingham. In the barbershop in the village that day, they got a newspaper, the only newspaper this village ever got. There it was spread out in front of the barbershop and all the villagers were reading it. On the front page was a picture of Bull Conner letting the dogs loose on the Black Christians praying in Birmingham, Alabama. Suddenly I discovered that the questions of racism and reaching unreached peoples are not two separate questions.

In 1890 the Southern Presbyterian Church sent to the Congo a man who had learned these things. William Henry Shepherd spent twenty years in Africa. Respected by the Africans, he was called 'Shoppit Monine, the Great Sheppard.' Working among the Bokuba people, he showed a cultural respect and sensitivity for things Africans had seldom seen among missionaries of his day. He knew how large this simple gospel was.

The Jesus that he preached was revolutionary in African society. For example, he resisted the custom of killing a slave to accompany a recently deceased master. He protested against the practice of trial by poison. When the Belgian government imposed a heavy food tax on the people, he protested. The tax forced the Africans to work for Europeans to pay it, a subtle form of colonialism. In addition, the government used soldiers who were cannibals to collect the tax. Shepherd discovered that the tax-collecting efforts were a cover for slave raids and for cannibalism. His protests brought the entire issue to the attention of King Leopold of Belgium. Strained relations with the government and with his mission finally brought him back to the States in retirement in 1910.

Sheppard had gone to Africa when the White Churches had almost no interest in Africa for Christ. Sheppard was Black, one of the 113 American Blacks who served in Africa from 1877 to 1900.

Who can tell how many Bakubans heard the word of Christ and believed because they saw Sheppard standing for the oppressed and the sinned against. How many there saw Sheppard himself as one of those sinned against? Could it have been that which brought them to Jesus Christ and to the cross?

What deed done for Christ will yet stir the hearts of the urban world's unreached peoples to hear the word spoken by Christ? And who will speak it and who will go to do it?

Harvie M. Conn, former missionary in Korea, is lecturer in missions and director of the urban missions programme at Westminster Theological Seminary in Philadelphia, USA.

Notes

[1]Gerd Theissen, *The Social Setting of Pauline Christianity* (T. & T. Clark, 1982. US ed. Philadelphia: Fortress, 1982), pp.74–75.
[2]Wayne Meeks, *The Moral World of the First Christians* (SPCK, 1987. US ed. Philadelphia: Westminster, 1986), pp.113–14.
[3]Quoted in Harvie M. Conn, *A Clarified Vision for Urban Mission* (Grand Rapids: Zondervan, 1987), p.162.
[4]Viv Grigg, 'Sorry! The Frontier Moved,' *Urban Mission* 4, no. 4 (March 1987), p.13.

6
CONCERN FOR THE MASSES
LUIS PALAU

To be faithful to the masses we must first have a passion for the masses. In 1 Timothy 2:1–4 Paul says, 'I urge, then, first of all, that requests, prayers, intercession and thanksgiving be made for everyone ... This is good, and pleases God our Saviour, who wants all men to be saved and to come to a knowledge of the truth.' Here are two thoughts. First, because God our Saviour wants all men to be saved, it pleases him that we should pray for all people. Second, he wants all people to come to a knowledge of the truth, the truth that 'there is one God and one mediator between God and men, the man Christ Jesus, who gave himself as a ransom for all men' (vv. 5–6).

In 1962 I came to Detroit to study and be a missionary intern for nine months. While I was there a missionary from what was then West Pakistan, Mr Montgomery, laid a burden on us for his land. At that point I didn't have much of a burden for that country. But he gave us a name of one Muslim man who had accepted Christ and who was being persecuted. And I put that name in my Amplified New Testament, which I still have at home. I have prayed for that man all these years. I don't know if he's still alive, of if he's in Heaven with the Lord; I have no idea. But the burden that Mr Montgomery laid on us at the conference at Highland Park Baptist Church turned my life around. And I began to feel a passion for the masses of West Pakistan.

How to eat an elephant

Now the thing that gets you when you think of the masses is the sheer enormity of it. As they say, how do you eat an elephant? One bite at a time. It's the only way. Although it's a massive beast, and there's a lot of meat in an elephant, if you really plan to eat it, there's only one way to do it. One bite at a time. And when you look at the masses of the world who are without Christ, you've got to start somewhere: where you are. I heard Elisabeth Elliot once say, 'Always do the next thing.'

If you want to get a passion and a burden for the masses, the first step, in my opinion, is to do what the Lord Jesus did. The Bible says in Matthew 9:36 that 'when he saw the crowds, he had compassion on them, because they were harassed and helpless, like sheep without a shepherd.' In other words, first we have to *look at them*.

Once, I was in a hotel in London waiting to get a bus to go to the airport with my sons Kevin and

Keith. The twins were about ten at the time. As we were sitting in the lobby, there were people from all races coming in and out. There were Muslims and Sikhs and ordinary Britishers and Americans. We were bored, so I thought I'd teach the boys about noticing people. I began to watch the people walking by and made comments about each one. And I said, 'Boys, what do you think that bellboy is thinking?' He was looking at the change that some guy had given him over the suitcases, and he looked mad. I said, 'I bet you he's saying "Cheapskate, stupid American"', and then the boys just began to laugh. Then came an Arab who looked like a sheik with a long, white robe and beard, and I said, 'What do you think he's thinking?' And we began to try to guess what people were thinking by looking at their faces. As people hustled in, sweaty with their bags or hassled by the employees at the counter, we just sat there and had the greatest fun – not judging people, but trying to guess what was going on.

When I was seventeen and just beginning to follow the Lord, I used to love to sit in the coffee shops with a magazine and a cup of coffee, just watching and listening to people. In airports I still like to do that. Just listen to people. You hear things; you watch people's reactions; you see couples fighting; you see kids hassling their parents; you see couples just kissing and carrying on. You see all sorts of things in airports. And one way I get turned on to masses is just watching them and trying to second-guess what's going through their minds. And although this might not work for you, it does me a lot of good. Because as I look at their eyes and their faces and try to read their body language, I try to get into their souls, and it is there where you find compassion.

One man particularly taught me a passion for the masses. Keith Benson was a missionary to Argentina from California. He was a fiery fellow. One day he invited me to pray with him. We set aside every Wednesday after work to pray. I was so excited. I must have been about twenty-two.

We got on our knees and he pulled out a map. He said, "Luis, we're going to pray for your church today – first Wednesday." And he'd learn by memory the names of the elders of my church, even though he didn't belong to it. He learned the names of my mother, my five sisters and my little brother.

He had a passion for prayer. I've prayed with a good number of men and women who really pray – I mean they really pray. But Keith Benson was the first. He would pray and talk to the Lord as if the Lord needed information. It was part of his style. For instance, he would say 'Lord, you know Mrs Palau is a widow. Lord, bless Mrs Palau.' And he'd carry on informing the Lord about every one of my sisters, Monty, Martha, Kim, Margaret, Ruth and my little brother George and about all sorts of things.

He'd pray up a storm and then stop. I had been brought up in both Brethren and Anglican churches, so I prayed too and covered all the territory I knew and said 'amen,' figuring that would be the end. But he would launch out into a second prayer. And he would pray then for the elders of my church and really lay it on the Lord. And then he'd get up and walk around still praying for neighbours, families and church leaders. The next Wednesday he showed up with a map of Córdoba, which is a city of about a million people, and there were about sixteen Brethren assemblies marked in blue on it. He'd start praying for each assembly. Now this wasn't a quicky prayer while you're shaving; these were long prayers. He'd point his finger at the map, 'Lord, here's an assembly ... Lord, I don't know the elders in that church but ...' and he'd go down and around the map. When he was finished, I felt that we had taken a ride around the city.

The next week he came with the same map, but besides the blue dots there were red dots – the Baptists. Benson knew them all. I prayed with him haltingly at first. But soon I began to pray a little more. I learned to pray for people – not just say a quick prayer to get it over with. I learned to enjoy prayer.

The next Wednesday he came with a map indicating all the Assemblies of God churches. Then he brought different maps, and we'd pray for all sorts of things. We'd pray for two to two-and-a-half hours. He'd get up for a little bit, but he'd never stop praying.

Next he came with a map of the whole province of Córdoba. He knew all the towns in the province, and he knew how many had churches. He would start praying from south to north, which was his habit. 'Lord, I've never been in this town, but there's a church there,' and he'd begin to pray. Then the next Wednesday he came with a map of all Argentina, and he'd start praying province by province, though not in so much detail.

Do you know what this did for me? It expanded my soul. I suddenly began to pray for people far beyond Córdoba and my little assembly and the twelve kids in my Sunday-school class. Suddenly we were really praying.

Then of course, you can imagine, he came with a map of South America, and we prayed country by country. One day he brought a globe, and we prayed continent by continent. Finally, he grabbed the globe and said, 'Lord, I love the world!' And oh, I tell you, that really moved me. I *knew* he loved the world.

One way to expand your heart and to begin to get a burden for the masses and a desire to do something about it is to pray. I really don't know any other way. Faithfulness to the masses has to begin with prayer. Obviously, we can't go everywhere. Single-handedly we can't convert all the Muslims, Buddhists, Hindus and all the other masses. But one thing we can do is to intercede in the power of the Holy Spirit. And then, under God, we decide 'where does the Lord want me?' God will show us the little corner of the world where he wants us to be.

Eternity and the masses
Faithfulness to the masses must remind us about eternity. Eternity is the most awesome thing in the world. Yes, we all get shaken up about hunger, war, torture, killing. But eternity should move us much more strongly. I believe that the passion God wants us to have for the masses comes when you think of the awesomeness of eternity. People die fat and people die hungry. People die in rich countries and people die in Third World countries. Everybody has to face eternity. Whether you are rich or poor, whether you are hungry or you are stuffed, you still have to face eternity. And a passion for the masses

comes when we realize that men and women outside of Christ are lost forever.

Dr R.A. Torrey said there are three steps in getting a passion for the masses: *studying* what the Bible has to say about the lost, *believing* it, and then *dwelling* on this truth until it takes hold of our hearts and we realize its meaning. In other words, we have to give ourselves time to let it sink in. Men and women outside of Christ are lost; and if we don't go out to them, they will die without Christ. And if they die without Christ, they are lost. Now the Judge of all the earth shall do right, I'm not concerned about that. But I am concerned about doing what I'm supposed to do, and dwelling on this gives me my burden.

I want to share with you about Dr Kraft and his son, David, and how they renewed in me a vision for the reality of heaven and the reality of eternity. Dr Kraft is the minister of Twin Lakes Baptist Church in Santa Cruz, California. David, his only son, went to Biola College, a typical young fellow that a father would love. David loved the Lord, enjoyed everything in college, liked girls, had fun, played basketball, and so on. After college he got married to a great gal and settled into the Bay Area.

When they were expecting their second child, David began to have some physical ailment. He went to the doctor, but the doctor couldn't figure out what it was. It got worse and worse and neither medicine nor prayer nor anything seemed to do anything for him. He was only thirty-two.

He had directed a camp for kids in the summer. People loved him. His dad loved him. Everybody loved Dave Kraft. Then there was nothing they could do; they took him to the hospital in Santa Cruz.

When I went to a missions conference there just a few years ago, the deacons said to me, 'We've really got to pray for Dr Kraft. He's so shaken by David.' David was plugged into all sorts of cables, and he was being kept alive on a life-support system, but he was totally awake.

The Sunday morning I was supposed to speak, I saw Dr Kraft. He seemed so relaxed. So I went up to him and I said, 'Dr Kraft, how's David?'

He said, 'Last night he went to be with the Lord.'

We were walking into the stadium to the platform, so I sat down beside him and began to think how I could comfort him. While the song service was going on I leaned over and said, 'Dr Kraft, I am really sorry. What shall we do this morning?'

He said, 'Let me tell you something.' And while the song service was going on, he told me this. He said, 'Last night I went to the hospital with my twin brother Roy. We prayed together and afterward David said to my brother, "Uncle, could you leave the room? I want to talk to Dad alone." When Roy left the room, David said, "Dad, come over here and give me a hug."

'I went over, knelt by the bed and put my arms around him. And David said to me, "Dad, I'm going to go home tonight."

'I looked at him and said, "Dave, you lucky guy. I thought I was going to beat you to it, but you'll beat me."

'And he said, "Dad, I want you to tell Mom how much I love her and tell her thanks. I want to thank you for the example you've been to me, I want to thank you for teaching me how to love the Lord Jesus, and I want to thank you for the way you have lived."

'"Dave, you lucky guy, to think that tonight you're going to heaven, and you're going to see Abel and Moses and Joshua. Can you imagine, Dave, you're going to see Daniel and David and St Paul. But best of all, you're going to see the Lord Jesus. And when you see him, tell him tonight, that your father loves him very much."

'We hugged each other, and I prayed for him. I went home after a little while and at about four o'clock in the morning, the doctor called and told me that David had just died. That's why I'm so relaxed this morning. Because Dave is in the presence of the Lord.'

And that's why we must be faithful to the masses. Because a man who dies with Christ as his Saviour has the assurance of eternal life and the reality of heaven here and in eternity. And that ought to shake us to care for the masses, to be faithful to the masses and to proclaim the message of the gospel. Because there are so many millions who are hungry to know the reality of eternal life.

Luis Palau heads an international evangelistic team which has held crusades throughout North, Central and South America; the West Indies; Europe and Australia. He has written books in Spanish and English, including Heart after God, The Luis Palau Story *and* Our God Reigns.

7
CONCERN FOR THE CITIES OF THE WORLD

RAY BAKKE

When I moved into Chicago in 1965, I read everything I could to help me make the transition to a community ridden with gangs and riots during the Vietnam era. I had been studying Scripture since I was a child. But the people who believed the Scripture were fleeing the city about as fast as those who didn't believe it. And I was confused by the cultural captivity of the urban church. So I read everything I could. *The Secular City* of Harvey Cox came out the same month that I moved into Chicago. Shortly thereafter, Jacques Ellul's book *The Meaning of the City* appeared. Somewhere between Cox's optimism and Ellul's pessimism, I thought, must lie the truth.

I picked up a radical theological journal and read that evangelicals and conservatives could not make it in the city. The reason, said the author, was that they take the Bible too literally. The Bible, said the author, is a rural book. God makes gardens; evil men make cities. God's favourite people are shepherds. His second favourite are vinegrowers. His least favourite are urban dwellers. Those of us who accept and take in Scripture, said the author, are swallowing an anti-urban bias. I think that there's an element of truth to this. But heresies, said William Temple, tend to be exaggerations of truths. Nonetheless, that thesis challenged me to get into Scripture like I never had before. I'd memorized Scripture for my personal growth. I had memorized Scripture in seminary to take hold of the great covenants and doctrines of God. But now I was driven to Scripture to see if there was in fact a theology as big as my city of Chicago. And I testify: indeed there is.

The city in the Old Testament

I found over one thousand references to cities in the Bible in both testaments. I found over one hundred cities listed in the Bible and began to do case studies on them. I started analysing the careers of biblical characters. Joseph was an Egyptian economist with two seven-year plans, one for budget surpluses and one for budget deficits. He was a man who urbanized the economy of Egypt and used the instruments of a pagan pharoah to feed the whole Middle East, including God's people. Read Genesis chapters 41 and 47 to see how he did it, combining elements both of socialism and capitalism.

I started looking at Moses with new eyesight. He was bi-cultural. Stephen in Acts said he was learned in all the wisdom of the Egyptians. With that culture and education Moses was then driven into the wilderness for field education: public health, primitive communities, sheep culture. After he married inter-racially, he was ready for ministry. He took a group of mud and brick makers from Egypt into the worst neighbourhood in the Middle East and built a culture for them. That is a pastoral model for a pastor in the large city.

I started looking at Nehemiah, that urban architect layman serving in the Persian government, who got a leave of absence and a government grant to go back and start the first biblical model-cities programme for the redevelopment of Jerusalem. The promise of Isaiah about the exiles who returned to Jerusalem applied to him: 'And you shall be called restorers of streets to dwell in.' If we are to faithfully face the cities of today, we have to recover a biblical theology for urban ministry.

I started looking at Daniel in the exile. Daniel 1:8 says, 'Daniel resolved not to defile himself.' Daniel sorted out the issues of faith and culture much like Niebuhr in this century. Daniel was able to master the king's curriculum yet reject the king's lifestyle and values. That is our task in the cities.

I started looking at the two books named for women in Scripture: Ruth, a commentary on the early history of Israel, and Esther, a commentary on the later history of Israel. Both are second marriages. Both deal with ethnicity but in different ways. One is assimilationist. One is dispersionist. I begin to see themes coming through the Scripture colourfully in ways I had never been taught.

I looked at Jonah, the urban missionary. According to a British author who over a hundred years ago wrote a marvellous little commentary called *Portrait of a Patriot*, 'The problem with Jonah is that he had wrapped the gospel in a Jewish flag.' He thought that because the Ninevites were his enemies, they were also God's enemies. He preached a certain amount of orthodoxy but with a heart that wasn't orthodox. He didn't love those people. He preached 'Repent or you'll go to hell.' And under his breath he was saying, 'I can hardly wait.' I've seen a lot of evangelism in Chicago and other places that's like that.

I started looking at the benefits of Diaspora Judaism. The fact that the Temple was destroyed was a great tragedy. But when those people were dispersed into the cities, they invented the synagogue and their faith became portable. They rediscovered the doctrine of angels. And more, they translated the Bible in Alexandria, Egypt, so that their children would learn the faith. The language issue arises over and over again in every generation among the immigrant groups in the cities.

I began to notice twenty-five kinds of urban ministry in the historical books of the Old Testament alone. Almost everything I would want the church to be doing in the cities today can be found in ancient Israel. Obviously we're going to have to become people of both testaments. We're going to have to do what the Reformers did – celebrate the theology of creation on the one hand and redemption on the other. Many of us have not been doing that. The dichotomy is tragic. It's cut us off from two-thirds of our Bible, much of which deals with cities.

The Jews dealt with crime by having cities of refuge directly run by priests. In fact, in looking through Deuteronomy, I found that the morality expected in the cities was higher than that expected in the countryside. If a woman was raped in the country, you stone the man. If she's raped in the city, you stone them both. Why? Because she should have screamed for help. Underneath that is a principle: the presence of people is presumed to have been beneficial.

I began to see in the Scripture how God looked at cities. Ezekiel chapter 16 is a classic passage on cities. God says Jerusalem's mother was a Hittite and her father was an Amorite (v. 45). See how families flow into places? There's no dichotomy between people and place in Scripture. It's what the biblical scholars call the corporate solidarity motif. It's an ecological theology that combines peoples and families. Listen how the prophet speaks of the city: 'Your older sister was Samaria, who lived to the north of you with her daughters (those are the suburbs and small towns indicating interdependency); and your younger sister, who lived to the south of you with her daughters, was Sodom' (Ezk. 16:46). Chicago, your sister to the north is Milwaukee; your sister in the south is Atlanta. Your cousin is Beirut, and Beirut hurts today. You should feel the pain in Chicago. There is no such thing in Scripture as throwaway environments. None at all. It is impossible to say that I love my city but that I hate another place, and still be a Christian biblically. You are Simon Bar-Jonah; you are Paul from Tarsus. Family and place are combined.

The city in the New Testament

I turned to the New Testament, and I found Jesus used the cities of Galilee. Matthew 9:35, a great missionary text, says he went about all the cities. He visited, taught, preached and healed. Then in chapter 10 he gives the mini-commission which anticipates the Great Commission. He sends the disciples out, but they were so wrapped with prejudice he didn't let them go outside the boundary of the country. The Holy Spirit hadn't yet come on them. And then in Matthew 11:1, after they came back and reported, he went back to the cities again. It's at the heart of Matthew.

Look also at Paul. E.M. Blaiklock, a late professor of New Testament, wrote a little book in 1968 called *Cities of the New Testament*. In the preface he said that the urban church followed the contours of the urbanized Roman empire. Stephen Neill, the late missionary, historian and theologian, in his book on the history of missions, says the early church was fortunate to have a person like Paul as the architect of its mission. Bicultural and multilingual, Paul went to the cities of the Roman empire. We have to recover that model.

This century has been called the century of homeless man. Perhaps ten million refugees wander the cities of the world. There's one book in the New Testament which is a private letter by Paul about an urban refugee, Onesimus. He stole money in Asia, ran away to Europe and found Christ in the ghetto. Paul had rented a house church in the Greek ghetto of south Rome where he was having a kind of Leighton Ford outreach campaign with his five Greek associates. Onesimus found Christ there and was sent back to Asia to be an evangelist, teacher and preacher.

The Bible may begin in a garden, but it ends in a city. We've got an urban future whether we like it or not. And what kind of a city is God building? Look at Isaiah chapter 58 which gives us a record. It's going to be a city with a housing policy, an employment policy and a public health policy, a city where the writer says the children do not die young. That's God's agenda and he's building a city right now. You couldn't honour him more, I suspect, than to love God and begin to love the city.

When Jeremiah wrote to the exiles who had been taken captive, they were living in a ghetto on the river called Kabar. They didn't like it. Their own city had been destroyed. But they got a letter from home that said that God had put them there (Je. 29:4). They thought,'What do you mean – "God put me here"? I got dragged here.' But the letter said they had been sent – on a mission. And then the prophet said they should put their roots in the city and raise their families there (Je. 29:5–6). And I challenge you to start doing that too. Stop running away from the cities. Move in there with your children. They'll be better off and so will you. I don't know where you can educate children who are any more realistic about the real world than in the cities of this country. Let's recover the Scripture, our biblical roots.

Recovering our historical heritage in the city

Wayne Meeks in his new book *The First Urban Christians* can give you some background. Robert

Banks's new book *Paul and Community: A Study of the Pauline House Churches* is a marvellous study of the New Testament churches in the city. E.M. Judge, writing twenty-five years ago on the social patterns of first-century Christian groups, said Christians were artisans, freedmen and slaves. And they went into the ghettoes of the Roman empire. I've read stories of those early Christians that I can hardly believe. Early Christians were garbage collectors, and they would pick up the bodies disposed among the Roman garbage and wash them and bury them. Why? Because they were the only people alive who believed in the resurrection.

In Alexandria, Egypt, according to some studies in the Philo Institute in Chicago, the diaconate emerged in the cities because women would send people down the streets to collect the unwanted babies that had been abandoned during the night. They would bring them to the public squares under the statues of Zeus, and there the women would nurse them, bathe them and catechize them. And that's how the church grew – through body hunts and baby hunts.

Mumford, in his classic book on the history of the city, has a chapter on how Christians ministered in the cities. He was no friend of an evangelical witness, but Mumford, who wrote over two dozen books summarizes his scholarship in this way: Christians didn't minister out of images of success. They would go into the city and look for occasions of misery. They looked for the sick, and they would offer to move in and live with them until they got well, often dying of the illnesses that they had come to seek and to serve.

There's more. In the Epistle to Diognetus, written

about AD 140, we read that Christians are to the world what the soul is to the body. Christians obey the laws of the land, and they far exceed them. Christians are the conscience of the cities. He goes on to extol all the ways in which the Christians were living 110 years after the cross in the Roman cities. It is an astounding list. And when you come to the end of chapter 6 you read this verse: 'To no less a post than this hath God ordered them, and they dare not try to evade it.'

Tertullian of Carthage, a lawyer, writing about AD 200, said to the emperor about the Christians: 'We have filled up every place belonging to you – islands, castles, caves, senates, prisons, palaces, senate forum. We leave you your temples only.' That was marvellous penetration by the church. Almost everything the early church did we need to be doing today. We not only need to recover our biblical roots; we need to discover our historical roots. I discovered an interesting fact one day when reading Latourette's description of the period from AD 500–1500, a period of a thousand years in which the church did not grow. In real estate and in warm-blooded believers, it was about the same in 500 as in 1500. But things had changed. We had lost Africa and we had gained Europe. Look more closely, and you will see that we lost African urban churches and gained European rural ones. All of which made me think that maybe today the church-growth statistics aren't measuring the metro picture. We may in fact be gaining suburbs and losing the cities.

I am a Scandinavian. The name *Bakke* means 'little mountain'. Do you know my history? It took a thousand years to make a Scandinavian Baptist. It started in 834. Anskar came across the Baltic. With the peace of God and the truce of God they sublimated the violence of us Vikings. We drove it inward. We have high suicide rates now. But at least we don't run around and kill everybody else. They made cultural Roman Catholics out of us. All of the strategies of the north European Middle Ages ought to be looked at for work in violent cities like my community today. We could learn. There's no need to reinvent that wheel. Then we became Lutherans, of course, and finally some Lutheran pietists came and taught our folks how to read the Bible. They discovered something about baptism. So in 1848, 1,014 years after Anskar, they baptized themselves and were promptly put in prison. It took 1,014 years to make a Swedish Baptist.

Something about that perspective needs to inform the way we approach the cities of today. It is not going to happen overnight. Some of you are interested in a reformation. Read Steven Ozment. Read Bernd Moeller. They are classic writers on the urban reformation. You will discover that Calvin pastored a city which increased forty per cent with refugees coming from all over Europe. And what did he do about it? He assigned the deacons to monitor the public-health hospital in Geneva to make sure that the poor refugees were being served. Maybe we've concentrated on church history as heroes and beliefs; we've not seen what was really going on.

There's more. When I was twenty-three as a young pastor in Seattle, I read about Charles Simeon, the Anglican whose story Inter-Varsity published back in 1948 when they reprinted the 1892 H.C.G. Moule edition called *Charles Simeon*. It changed my life. It gave me a vision of an urban church and an urban pastor. It is still my model for what a church and a ministry can be and ought to be in the city.

Shaftesbury died a hundred years ago this coming year. He was a layman who took a verse out of Corinthians and organized the London Water Board to deliver potable water to the Dickens London slums. And he did many other things as well.

Let me talk about women. On September 21, 1889, two women, Julia and Jane, walked down the streets of the worst slum in Chicago and bought an old house. Jane's father had just died. She was a graduate of Rockford Women's Seminary where she had learned Greek, her favourite subject. So she moved into the old Greek barrio of Chicago near the Italian slum. A short time later she was sleeping in her upper room, and a burglar came through the window. She was terrified. She pretended to be asleep and lay there while the burglar ransacked everything. He was about to go back out the window when in her frightened way she said, 'Why don't you use the stairs? You might get hurt.'

The burglar came over to the bed and sat down and started to cry. 'I have just been promoted to second-storey burglary, and I have blown it.' He told her about the poor life he had led. Jane Addams went out the next day and got him a job. I question a lot of things about her theology, but not about her methodology and her ability to take risks.

In 1893 William Stead wrote a book, *If Christ Came to Chicago*, about Gipsy Smith and the evangelicals who took on the Levee, the red-light district. Everything you could imagine in the twentieth century was

101

for sale in the Levee in the nineteenth century. If you turn to the appendix of that book you'll find, surprisingly, that the evangelicals were also on the urban clean-up committee. The committee was chaired by a Unitarian. But if you look down the list at the executive committee, you'll find R.A. Torrey, president, Moody Bible Institute. Evangelicals in those days weren't afraid to take risks. Those of you from an Alliance tradition should preach salvation in the slums and learn about A.B. Simpson. You have urban roots too. Many times we've forgotten our roots, and we've forgotten our Scriptures.

The changing city

Let me turn to the modern world. It is growing at the rate of about two Chicagos a month. It is producing cities growing at the rate of 7.2% a year. It will double in the next ten to fifteen years. Mexico City had eighteen million people as of January 1984. It is growing at the rate of eighty thousand a month, a million a year – a little over half of which is made up of newborns. Put another way, a city the size of Seattle is *born* in Mexico City every year. At the same time a city larger than Milwaukee *moves* into Mexico City every year. The cities of the United States have a median age of about 31 . . . and rising. We in the West are aging. The median age in Mexico City is 14.2. Nine million children. Do you see any implications for missions?

There are at least three major ways cities are different today from in the past. First, while cities today continue to have an incoming population, they are built on an exploding birthrate. Second, the cities are running out of air and water. Third, they are shifting from labour- to capital-intensive economies; so they're running out of jobs. Scholars are talking not only about unemployment but even more about how explosive under-employment is. What one African has called a social time bomb is about to go off. Rising expectations, what sociologists call push factors and pull factors, are bringing people to cities like gigantic magnets. Yet when they get there the jobs disappear and people who are cut loose from their roots and the stability of tribal cultures are finding themselves in cities with no place to turn.

Not so long ago a mouse ran down my street. And all of a sudden there was a 'meow.' So the mouse jumped into a manhole. But he couldn't quite get away because it was full of water. So he stayed on a brick. Unfortunately, the cat couldn't quite reach down there. He was just scratching the top of the mouse's fur. Suddenly there was a 'Ruff, ruff, ruff!' and the scuffling of padded feet. Then it was quiet. Thinking the cat had been chased by a dog, the mouse came up, started looking around (you know how arrogant urban mice are) and suddenly, whop! It was the cat.

The cat was about to eat the mouse when the mouse said, 'Wait a minute! Wait a minute! Where's the dog?'

'Mouse,' said the cat, 'if you're going to survive in the cities, you've got to be bilingual.'

What John Stott has called the polychrome church of God is alive and well in the cities of the world. There are now two hundred and fifty cities with a million or more people. In sixteen years there will be five hundred cities with a million or more people.

Into them God is calling some of you. God has called some of you elsewhere. But we have to reach these great cities. Some mission agencies probably should not split their resources and come into the city. There are still a billion people that are distantly unreached. But we're talking about the rapidly-growing, culturally-unreached within the shadows of our own building.

I live in a one-mile square of sixty thousand people. Fifty nations are represented in the public school which our children attend. There are many different languages. We have two hundred and twenty-three nations in the world and fifty of them are in my one-mile square. In May 1982 the *New York Times* did a study of Chinatown, and they said this: All of the provinces of mainland China can now be found with immigrants living in a four-block territory of New York City. That is urban reality. Houston is now eighty per cent Black, Hispanic and Asian in the public school system. The largest Mexican city is Mexico City, but the second largest is Los Angeles. And that's the way the world is turning.

In Europe the empire strikes back. London was head of the world. Now the world is in London; the world is in Berlin; the world is in Europe. It's wonderful how God is moving the world around.

Slowly the world is turning from an Atlantic to a Pacific perimeter, being attracted by these gigantic cities in Asia. It will affect the way we live, the way we spend money, the politics of our country and everything else in our future. We have to respond.

I know you want me to be practical, but I'm going to close with a story that is perhaps a little irresponsible. But I'm going to do it anyway.

In 1914 the Germans were sinking US shipping in the North Atlantic. It was a turkey shoot because the Germans had the U-boat and we didn't. Somebody asked the American folk philosopher Will Rogers what we ought to do about it. He thought about it for a moment and said, 'Well, I think you should boil the ocean.'

The man was incredulous. 'Boil the ocean?'

'Yes,' said Rogers. 'I think if you heated up the Atlantic ocean, the submarines would rise to the surface and you would capture them.'

'But how do you boil an ocean?' the man asked.

Rogers responded, 'I've given you the solution. It's up to you to work out the details.'

Ray Bakke, author of The Urban Christian *(MARC Europe, 1987), lectures in ministry at Northern Baptist Theological Seminary and is senior and associate international co-ordinator for the Lausanne Committee for World Evangelization.*

8
WHERE DO WE GO FROM HERE?

PETER MAIDEN

Books and conferences on urban evangelism are now increasing. Praise God! We need to think, study and pray. But let's be careful we do not begin and end here. God loves the people of the cities of the world. The longing of Jesus for the city of Jerusalem was clear for all to see.

'God so loved the world that he gave'. God's love is a giving love – the only true love. Do I share God's love for the cities? What am I willing to give?

I write these words in Amsterdam. Floyd has already shared something of the enormous need and opportunity of this city. Parts of Amsterdam fill me with revulsion. My natural reaction is to want to pack my bags and go home. God's final words to Jonah about Nineveh, however, come to mind:

'Should I not be concerned about that great city?'

How did God express his concern for Nineveh? He sent a man with a message. Surely that's what Amsterdam, Jakarta, Chicago and London need. God's men and women with a message.

God with us

Cities need people, God's people, who will be salt and light in these places. The model of God's incarnation has already been mentioned in this book: 'The Word became flesh and made his dwelling among us' (Jn. 1:14). That was God's method to reach us – not to preach to us from a distance, not an occasional rushed visit. He became one of us and identified himself with us – sitting where we sit, suffering what we suffer, dying our death. This was also Paul's method: 'We loved you so much that we were delighted to share with you not only the gospel of God but our lives as well' (I Thes. 2:8).

Are we ready to share our lives with the people of the cities? The only authentic mission is incarnational mission.

I worked for a number of months with a small church whose members told me that they wanted to see growth in their church. I began to go from door to door in the streets in the immediate vicinity of the church, interested to discover what the local people thought about the church. They had little idea what it was. 'Twice on a Sunday', one person said, 'people arrive – many in large cars, they disappear within for about one and a half hours, then emerge and get back in their vehicles and off they go.' These people were certainly preaching a message, but were they giving their lives?

A model for our message

Cities need models as well as a message, those which people can copy and thereby become imitators of Christ. As well as model Christian homes in the city, Christians are needed who will live out the full implication of the gospel, both as employers and employees. Cities need God's people living in them, identifying with the people of the city.

Cities need people with a message – God's message. Our message is new relationships. Alienation through sin is dealt with by Christ. We are 'no longer foreigners and aliens, but fellow-citizens with God's people and members of God's household, built on the foundation of the apostles and prophets, with Christ Jesus himself as the chief cornerstone. (Eph. 2:19).

In Christ the homeless come home, the disinherited come into their inheritance. We must permeate the cities of our world with this message of hope.

Into action

Is our action going to end with books and conferences, or are we going to take the challenge of the city personally and seriously?

What can you do? Pray for a city. Ray Bakke assures us that by the year 2000 there will be nearly 5000 cities of 1 million or more people. Adopt one of these great cities. Find out the facts. What are the specific needs? Who is working there? Maybe you should visit that city. Begin serious and consistent intercession for one of the world class cities.

The 10 largest cities in the year 2000

1. Mexico City, Mexico – 26 million
2. São Paulo, Brazil – 24 million
3. Tokyo/Yokohama, Japan – 17.1 million
4. Calcutta, India – 16.6 million
5. Greater Bombay, India – 16 million
6. New York/North East New Jersey, USA – 15.5 million
7. Seoul, Republic of Korea – 13.5 million
8. Shanghai, China – 13.5 million
9. Rio de Janeiro, Brazil – 13.3 million
10. Delhi, India – 13.3 million

Could you encourage your church into a twinning arrangement with a church in one of those world class cities? Prayer, giving to a mission working in that city or a church there, visits to and from the city, could be encouraged. Renewal in our own churches may well be a marvellous by-product.

This book has shown that many of these great cities will be in areas of the world where the witness of the church is weakest. The Islamic world will be home to some of the greatest of these cities. God is surely calling some of us to move from our country and culture and invest our lives in these cities.

Probably 'missionary' will not be in our passport – teacher, engineer perhaps – but we will be there for the name and sake of Christ.

A variety of missionary societies are launching programmes to meet specific needs in the cities. For example, *Love Europe* has as one of its main objectives to see the Word of God made available to the people of the great cities of East and West Europe. There is a famine of God's Word in the great cities of the world. You can help to change that situation.

Finally, don't flee the city – the natural drift for many Christians is to be out of the city. Ask God if it is his will for you to move into the city? If by the year 2000 the church is in the suburbs, we will have distanced ourselves from over half the world's people.

Peter Maiden assists George Verwer in the International Co-ordination of Operation Mobilisation, and is involved in a major initiative in mission, Love Europe, *run by OM.*

PART II
A BIBLE
EXPOSITION

Ajith Fernando

9
GOD'S CONCERN FOR A CITY: JONAH'S CALL TO NINEVEH
AJITH FERNANDO

Running away from God (Jonah 1:1–16)

The book of Jonah begins by saying, 'The word of the Lord came to Jonah son of Amittai.' Who is this man Jonah? He lived at the time in the Jewish nation when it was divided into two groups. In the north was Israel, and in the south was the kingdom of Judah. Jonah was from the northern kingdom. He lived about the eighth century before Christ. He is mentioned in 2 Kings 14:25 as a prophet from Gath Hepher, who prophesied that Jeroboam the king of Israel would restore the boundaries of Israel, and it was fulfilled during his own lifetime.

Obviously Jonah was a person with some respect in society.

Jonah's strange commission

Verse 1 tells us that 'the word of the Lord came to Jonah.' This is a common biblical way of saying that God had communicated his message to his prophet. How exactly it was communicated we are not told. Perhaps it was done in different ways at different times – through dreams, through visions, through a strong impression in the mind of the prophet – and it came to be called the word of the Lord.

Verse 2 tells us that the word of the Lord to Jonah said, 'Go to the great city of Nineveh and preach against it, because its wickedness has come up before me.' This is a very hard commission. No prophet before had been sent to the streets of another nation to preach judgment. Elijah was sent to other nations but never with a message like this.

Nineveh was quite a distance away, probably over six hundred miles as the crow flies, and about seven hundred and fifty miles by road. Jonah would probably have had to walk. It was a very big city. Here was a lone person from another country asked to go and make contacts there and to preach against this city – a very difficult task.

As a Jew, Jonah must have had all sorts of problems about going and preaching to Gentiles. There were theological blocks that prevented him from doing this – we are told that Nineveh was a wicked city. They were enemies of Israel, and they were very well known for the ways in which they were cruel to their enemies. Jonah was asked to go and preach against this city.

There is a cartoon by Kurt Mitchell in a children's book that expresses Jonah's dilemma very well. In this cartoon Jonah is depicted as a mouse and the people of Nineveh as cats. This mouse is asked to go and preach to the cats. Someone has said it was like asking a Jewish rabbi in 1943 to go to Berlin and cry against the wickedness of the people there – a very hard job.

But the call of God is often like this. It takes us to places which others regard as impossible, to do work which looks like utter folly. Of course, with the call of God comes God's provision, but we don't always see that at the start.

World evangelism today

The work of world evangelism looks something like this at the end of the twentieth century. What we think of as sacrificial service, the world regards as arrogant imposition. Christians in Sri Lanka, for example, are embarrassed by our historical connections with the colonial rulers. Non-Christians and even some Christians think that evangelism is an extension of this colonial spirit – the same spirit of arrogance that tries to impose our will on others. It's nothing of the sort! But that's the way people think about it. Also, the world's religions are experiencing a resurgence now, and they too have developed a missionary zeal. So ours is not an easy call.

Just a few weeks ago we had a very unusual meeting, and the majority of the people there were Hindus. My colleague who was preaching presented very clearly the message that Christ is unique and that he is the only saviour. A section of the audience was so enraged by what he said that they wanted to

117

assault him. But a few of those who attended heard the message, accepted it and gave their lives to Christ.

Sometimes the temptation comes to us to downplay evangelism, for it implies the need for people to discard their old ways and to follow Jesus Christ as their only saviour. But we must not and we cannot downplay evangelism if we are obedient to God.

The call of Jonah was costly, just as our call will be costly. The Lord will teach us to preach against the city because its wickedness has come up before him.

This expression, *preaching against the city*, suggests that we are to present God as a judge who has been sinned against. This is a familiar theme in the Scriptures. We preach to people not only because we have good news that God loves people – that is our primary message – but also because people's sins have come up against God, because they are lost and heading for judgment. We must not forget this fact.

Running from God

In verse 3 we are told that Jonah ran away from the Lord and headed for Tarshish. Tarshish is probably Tartessus, a town in Spain. It was a town far west of Palestine, on the western edge of the world they knew about. Nineveh was on the eastern edge of the world they knew about. Jonah was asked to go to the far eastern edge of their world, but he went to the far west.

Now you might ask, 'Why didn't Jonah stay in the comfort of his home in Palestine? If he wanted to disobey God, why did he have to go all the way to Tarshish?' Tarshish was a place where you would least expect a revelation from God. The people there didn't know the Lord. Being disobedient to God is extremely uncomfortable, and when you're disobedient to God and meet God's people, you become even more uncomfortable. So Jonah wanted to be a safe distance from anything that reminded him of God.

In the second part of the verse we are told that Jonah went to Joppa, and he found a ship bound for the port of Tarshish. After paying the fare, he went on board and sailed for Tarshish to flee from the Lord.

Jonah's humiliation

According to verse 4, the Lord sent such a violent storm on the sea that the ship threatened to break up. Jonah had tried to run away from God, but all he succeeded in doing was forfeiting the peace of God's presence. Then suddenly he had to face the power of God's presence! God was there, and he showed himself in great power.

We are told in verse 5 that all the sailors were afraid, and each one cried to his own god. When their prayer didn't seem to work, they were forced to do something a little more costly – they threw out the cargo to lighten the ship, but that, too, didn't work.

In the third part of verse 5 we are told: 'But Jonah had gone below deck, where he lay down and fell into a deep sleep.' While the Gentiles are desperately seeking a solution – but looking in the wrong place – the servant of the living God, who knows the solution, is fast asleep.

Possibly Jonah was exhausted after running fast

to Joppa to get away from the presence of the Lord – but what a sad sight! The people of this world are looking desperately for an answer, and they don't know where to go or what to do, and the one who knows the answer is asleep! What criminal negligence, we would say.

But could that be said of us too? Living in a world of such need, we who have found the One who is the only answer to that need are in the slumber of our disobedience!

The captain went to him and said, 'How can you sleep? Get up and call on your god! Maybe he will take notice of us, and we will not perish.' What a humiliating awakening for this servant of God, this respected prophet of the Lord. He is not being persecuted for his failure. He is not being ridiculed for his beliefs. He is being justifiably scolded by an unbeliever for being in the wrong place.

The servants of God are humiliated when they are caught in the wrong place because of their disobedience. For example, a Christian witness is humiliated when a person he has witnessed to sees him coming out of a pornographic book store. A Christian student is humiliated when she is caught cheating on a term paper. A Christian youth is humiliated when he is justifiably rebuked by his non-Christian parents for his own selfishness – a child of the light, justifiably rebuked by a child of darkness, an ambassador of the King of kings and Lord of lords, rebuked by one to whom he is supposed to introduce the King. What a contrast our call from Jesus is: 'Let your light shine before men, that they may see your good deeds and praise your Father in heaven' (Mt. 5:16).

The captain asked Jonah to pray to his god. He may have thought: the other gods have been tried; this god may have been left out. We don't know how Jonah responded to the captain's request. He may have just murmured something and sheepishly followed the captain to the deck.

The sailors said: 'Come, let us cast lots to find out who is responsible for this calamity.' They had tried prayer, and it didn't work. Then they tried throwing something away, and that didn't work. They seemed to have been convinced that there was something out of the ordinary in this storm. Perhaps they thought there was somebody responsible for this situation – someone with a curse on him. They said to themselves: 'A lot may reveal the guilty person.' So they cast lots, and the lot fell upon Jonah. The Lord sovereignly intervened, and Jonah was caught!

In verse 8 the sailors asked Jonah, 'Tell us, who is responsible for making all this trouble for us? What do you do? Where do you come from? What is your country? From what people are you?' These sailors were quite honourable people. There was a lot of desperation in their tone, but they didn't manhandle Jonah, they just questioned him.

Jonah answered, 'I am a Hebrew and I worship the Lord, the God of heaven, who made the sea and the land.' 'I am a Hebrew' – that's how neighbours identified Jews. 'I worship the Lord' – in the original Hebrew it was YHWH. There were no vowels in the original Hebrew, and when people added vowels they pronounced YHWH as 'Jehovah.' This was the specifically Israelite name of the Lord, his personal name. It was not used by others, so Jonah was describing God as the God of Israel.

The God of heaven

Jonah then goes on to describe God a little further. He says, 'the God of heaven, who made the sea and the land.' This word 'God' is from the Hebrew word *Elohim*, which was the common word for God in the ancient Near East. It is the word from which we get Allah, the word Muslims use for God. But he's not just any God, he is the 'God of heaven.' He is not just a local deity; he is the sovereign God. Jonah is trying to tell these people that this is the greatest God that there is. Then he expresses God's supremacy more clearly by stating that he made the sea and the land. He is the creator of everything. So the sailors realize then that nothing can stop this storm. The Creator himself is responsible.

This is the biblical way to introduce God to non-Christians. He is presented as supreme, and he is presented as Creator. This is how Paul, for example, introduced God when he was speaking in Lystra and Athens to the people who were not Christians, who had no biblical background. When we witness to Buddhists and Hindus in Sri Lanka, one of the first things we stress is the fact that God is the Creator. In our evangelistic camps in Youth for Christ the first session that we have is on the creation. That is the basic thing we need to establish.

I have a dear friend in Sri Lanka who was a devout Buddhist. A fellow student on campus told him about Jesus Christ and took him to an Inter-Varsity meeting. After he went to that meeting, he said that Christianity just didn't make any sense – especially the idea of Jesus Christ dying for the sins of other people. He just couldn't understand it. It seemed like nonsense until he realized that God is

Creator. When he realized that, everything else began to fall into place. Last month he was baptized as a Christian.

We see the effectiveness of this in the sailors' reaction in verse 10. We are told that when Jonah said this, it terrified them. The sailors had been frightened by the storm, but their fear becomes terror when they realize that they are dealing with the supreme God.

The evangelistic value of establishing the supremacy of God is very clear here. There are tremendous repercussions when a person becomes a Christian. All sorts of problems come. The new Christian wonders, 'Will my relatives go against me? Will all these people persecute me?' And they are afraid. Then we present to them the fact that God is the creator of the universe. He is supreme. He is greater than all the gods and the masters of this world. Therefore, if he is so great, the wisest thing to do is to follow him.

When Jonah told them that, they asked him, 'What have you done?' They were saying in effect, 'How could you do such a thing?' They were pointing out to Jonah the folly of his disobedience. What follows is a very interesting parenthesis: they knew he was running away from the Lord because he had already told them so. Why then didn't they scold him when he told them at the start?

In everyday life it is the obedient person, the one who pays the price of following God's ways, who looks like a fool. The world looks at the sacrifices we make, and they think we are fools. They feel sorry for us. The way of obedience results in victory, but for a moment it seems as if the way of obedience is a difficult way. God will ultimately reveal the real situation, but until then people see what looks like the folly of obedience.

That's what happened in Jonah's case. When Jonah first told them he was running away from the Lord, it did not strike them as something special. Then came the revelation of God in the storm, and they saw the facts as they were. They realized the folly of disobedience, and when they realized it, they said, 'What a fool you are!'

I hope this sobers us. So many people choose the path of folly because they think it's the best way. The way of obedience seems to cost too much. The price seems to be too high. They win acclaim on earth, but when the Lord reveals himself – and he will some day – we realize the folly of following the way of the world. 'The world and its desires pass away' says the apostle John, 'but the one who does the will of God lives forever' (1 Jn. 2:17).

Jonah faces up to his sin

The sea was getting rougher and rougher. So they asked Jonah, 'What should we do to you to make the sea calm down for us?' 'Pick me up and throw me into the sea,' he replied, 'and it will become calm. I know that it is my fault that this great storm has come upon you.' Jonah's godly character finally shines through. He is willing to die so that others on the ship will be saved. He has run away from God, he has nowhere to go. Now he says, 'Lord, take me.'

I wonder if this is why Jesus compared Jonah to himself. Jesus gave himself so that the world would live. Jonah gave himself so that the sailors might live. But these sailors prove to be too honourable to let Jonah die like that, so they try to row back to the land. Then the sea grows wilder than before. God was not going to short-circuit the process of Jonah's repentance. Jonah's sin was so serious that he had to face up to the full implication of his sin. There was no shortcut to his repentance. And Jonah had to face up to his sin before he received God's full restoration. Remember that.

Let me conclude by saying that the most prominent objection to Christianity I have heard from Buddhists and Hindus is: 'Your forgiveness is cheap. You receive God's forgiveness and live any way that you like.' The implication is that Christianity is cheap. They think their religion is more noble because they take sin seriously.

My dear friends, the Bible says God does take sin seriously, and we cannot trifle with it. This is the lesson God taught Jonah. It is the central theme of this passage. God is holy. We cannot run away from him. It is folly to try. If you are trying to run away from God, let me tell you that it is useless. All your excuses are too weak to stand the scrutiny of God's holy wisdom. Come back to him before it's too late. Don't wait for God to do something drastic like sending you to the bottom of the sea.

Praise for deliverance (Jonah 1:17 – 2:10)

Near the end of chapter one we find Jonah in a desperate state, thrown into the sea with no hope of survival. But the situation begins to change at 1:17 as God intervenes once more. Verse 17 states: 'But the Lord provided a great fish to swallow Jonah, and Jonah was inside the fish three days and three nights.'

We don't know what happened to Jonah the moment he was thrown out of his boat. Was he swallowed at once in a conscious state? Or had he half-drowned and lost consciousness? Some people even think he died. If he did lose consciousness, which is quite likely, he would have got quite a shock when he awoke. 'Is this the bottom of the sea? It's very dark but relatively dry. Is this Sheol, the place of the dead? Something fishy is going on here!' The truth would have finally dawned on him. He was still alive, and while there is life, there is hope. God had acted on his behalf.

Jonah's song of praise

Jonah 2:1 states: 'From inside the fish Jonah prayed to the Lord (Yahweh) his God.' Note the way the relationship with God is described: 'Yahweh his God.' Jonah is no longer running away from God. He is God's servant, enjoying an intimate relationship with God again, and his joy expresses itself in a prayer.

Jonah's prayer follows a pattern of a certain type

of psalm in the Bible that is given in response to God's salvation. The Jews used different types of prayers to help them respond to different situations. These prayers enabled them to make praise and thanksgiving part of their lifestyle. How often we neglect to thank God after a prayer is answered. We pray very hard to God, but when he answers we forget to thank him, because praise has not become part of our lifestyle.

Let me use a Sri Lankan example. One hot, humid day a lady came by bus to visit her sister. The bus dropped her in town, and she had a long walk to her sister's home. She walked in the hot sun with the beads of perspiration running down her. As she walked and entered the house, her nephew came and said, 'Auntie, my rubber ball broke yesterday. Would you please give me a new ball?'

The auntie turned, went back outside and walked to the centre of the town. After half an hour, she returned with the ball, tired and perspiring. The boy grabbed the ball from his aunt and ran away to play with it. Now we would rebuke that boy for ingratitude. But that's precisely what we often do when we don't stop to say thank you. The Jews had formal prayers to help them thank God. These had become part of their lifestyle.

Some of you may feel you have gone so far from God that there's no hope for you. Take heart! The Bible says that God will not despise a broken and a contrite heart. He heard the prayers of Jonah, and he can hear your prayer too!

Jonah's prayer includes a *renewed vow to praise God*. Look at verse 9: 'But I, with a song of thanksgiving, will sacrifice to you. What I have vowed I

127

will make good.' Jonah resolves to praise God. This type of resolve is very common in the Bible. These resolves address the will. They are deliberate decisions to praise God.

Sometimes praise does not come naturally to us. Our mood may not be right to praise God. Praise is not always a spontaneous outburst of our experience. Such outbursts may happen after exciting experiences, but we don't have exciting experiences every day. At times we need to address our wills and make a decision to praise God. That may sound like bondage, but it isn't. When we praise God, we are praising him for things that are eternally true. When we start praising God, we will find out that praise was what we wanted to do in our inner self. Our external mood did not spontaneously produce praise, but in our heart of hearts that's what we wanted to do.

Christianity is often like that. When I go to pray, I often don't feel like praying. But I decide to pray anyway, and when I begin I find that I deeply enjoy it!

Christianity is not a drudgery. Don't ever become a missionary because you feel guilty. Get involved in the world evangelization because you want to be obedient to God! When we are obedient to God, we open the door to experiencing his joy fully. When we have opened ourselves to that joy, whatever our trouble or suffering may be, there is a joy that is too deep for any of our troubles to reach. C.S. Lewis said that the whole mark of a Christian is not love, not even faith, but joy – joy because we are living with the King of kings and Lord of lords!

A song amid the gloom

How could Jonah have prayed a prayer like this from inside a fish? That's hardly a place to pray a song of deliverance! Some have rejected the idea that this psalm was sung from inside the fish. They say it was probably a later edition inserted in the wrong place by some editor. But is such a mistake probable?

Jacques Ellul points out that Jewish rabbis in the pre-Christian era were characterized by patience, competence, erudition and acuteness. Could such meticulous people have made such a glaring mistake of putting this in the wrong place? To accept this, says Ellul, is to regard the commentators who amended the text as imbeciles. If Jonah could not have prayed like this, the rabbis would have made some adjustments to make the text sound a little less silly. The prayer is there because obviously it is intended to be there.

How then could Jonah have prayed a prayer like this from inside the fish? Verse 1 gives us the key. Jonah prays to the Lord his God. Jonah's relationship with his God has been re-established. At the end of verse 1 we are told that he had accepted his sinfulness. Now he opens the door for God to come into him, and re-establishes his contact with grace. There is still gloom all around him physically, but a ray of light has crept through the clouds of darkness. That ray of light is, as it were, a guarantee of God's abounding sufficient grace. Jonah clings to that ray of light. With the eyes of faith, he sees the sunshine of God's grace behind the clouds. Jonah can sing a song of praise in the night because God is who he says he is, and Jonah knows the night will pass.

The same is true for us. When we feel surrounded by darkness, suddenly God will give us a little sense that he is still with us. That little sense is like a light that enters our experience and envelops us with hope. God is! God is still there, and God's grace is greater than every circumstance we face.

The miracle is completed with Jonah's release. Verse 10 states: 'And the Lord commanded the fish, and it vomited Jonah onto dry land.' The door is open once again for God to work with Jonah, to use him as his prophet.

It is striking that almost all the phrases in this psalm are from the Bible. Jonah's prayer reveals that he had memorized the Scriptures. He didn't have a Bible with him inside the fish, but he had one in his heart. If we want strength from God to face the crises of life, we need to be reading the Scriptures when we don't have the crises, when things are going fine. Psalm 119:11 says, 'I have hidden your word in my heart that I might not sin against you.' When a crisis comes, we might not have time to go and get a Bible. So God's Word needs to be stored in our hearts – ready for use – like water in a reservoir.

There is no magical formula, however, for memorizing Scripture. It comes through a regular, disciplined study of God's Word. If you have not begun such disciplined study, may you begin it. And if you have begun such study, may you long continue it.

Revival in Nineveh
(Jonah 3)

In Jonah 2 we saw how Jonah had been rescued and how grateful he was for being rescued. In Jonah 3 we see how Jonah is recommissioned and the ministry he carries out as a recommissioned person.

A second chance

'Then the word of the Lord came to Jonah a second time' (3:1). Jonah got a second chance. When did this happen? We don't really know. Perhaps it was the moment he set foot on dry land or some time later. We aren't told when, but we are told that he got a second chance.

Not everybody in the Bible gets a second chance. We have stories of prophets, for example, who disobey God and then cannot go back to their ministry. We should not assume we will get a second chance just because Jonah did. The Bible doesn't give us that assurance. So long as we are sensitive to God, we can come back to him. Sometimes, however, we close ourselves to God by our disobedience and thus block our way to restoration. It is dangerous to take chances with disobedience. God is too holy to make it safe for us to take risks with his will. Hebrews 10:31 says, 'It is a dreadful thing to fall into the hands of the living God.'

But the story of Jonah gives hope to anyone who realizes that he or she has moved away from God's will. If we return to God, he will accept us. Isaiah urges us to 'seek the Lord while he may be found;

call on him while he is near. Let the wicked forsake his way ... Let him turn to the Lord, and he will have mercy on him, and to our God, for he will freely pardon' (55:6–7).

A difficult call

In verse 2 the Lord says, 'Go to the great city of Nineveh.' This is the second time Nineveh has been described as a great city. Again this places emphasis on the immensity of the task before Jonah. This wasn't going to be an easy job. The Bible never downplays the difficult aspects of God's call. It is a glorious call, and with it comes adequate provision, but it is a hard call. Whether you follow Christ into the business world, or whether you're going to the mission field, it's going to be hard.

Consider the call into missionary service. There is the frustration of taking so much time to identify with the people to whom you're ministering. Many, therefore, choose not to identify. There is the disappointment of not being appreciated by the people you have come to serve. There are problems with fellow Christians. Some people who have trouble in their so-called secular jobs decide to go into Christian work because it is so much more pleasant. Well, they're in for a shock! Invariably it is going to be harder. If you want to be a missionary, don't go like a starry-eyed idealist. The shock of reality may be too difficult for you to take. You may go back disillusioned.

John Calvin said that the reason that the character of the city was mentioned 'was that Jonah might gird up himself for the contest, so that he might not afterward fail in the middle of his course.'

A message from God

The second part of verse 2 states that the Lord told Jonah to 'proclaim to it the message I give you.' Jonah was not too happy about this message, but it sparked a tremendous revival. Why? Obviously the people were prepared. Also, there was power in Jonah's message, because God told him to proclaim it.

This is the real romance of missions. We take a message to created people from their Creator. That is the most important thing they need to hear. That is the greatest of missions. We are taking the only message worth hearing to the people of the world – a message from their Creator.

The romance of missions is not the thrill of travel. After some time, you get tired of the sight of a suitcase. It is not the excitement of adventure, because the adventure soon wears off. It is not the joy of harvesting fruit, because some are called to work in unreceptive areas. They are called to open closed doors, to prepare barren fields for the seed. Others will enjoy the fruits of their work. It is not the fulfilment of using our gifts. One of the most beautiful aspects about Christian ministry is to use our gifts, to be useful, to know that God has given us a valuable contribution to make. But soon we realize our own inadequacy. We realize we are jars of clay.

But these jars of clay contain a treasure (2 Cor. 4:7). The Creator's message to this bewildered generation is the only hope they have. It is 'the power of God for the salvation of everyone who believes' (Rom. 1:16). No wonder Paul said that he's not ashamed of the gospel or, to put it positively, that he was excited about the gospel. Our message is a message from God. 1 Peter 4:11 states: 'If anyone speaks, he should do it as one speaking the very words of God.'

I work for Youth for Christ. Our primary focus is to proclaim Christ to young people who are out of contact with the church, young people who are not interested in Christianity. We have various types of programmes to attract these young people – sports, music, drama, adventure – all sorts of things just to make contact with the non-Christian youth.

At the end of these programmes we often preach the gospel, and usually I have the responsibility of doing this. For many of the youth, this is the least important part of the programme. Some of them walk away when I start speaking. When I get up to speak, I struggle with nervousness. I often feel like Daniel in the den of lions. But I have a confidence. This is not my message. This is the message of the King of kings and the Lord of lords, the Creator of these young people! This gives me confidence – confidence not in myself, but in the message, because it's the truth that will set these young people free. So let's stay close to the message, know it thoroughly, and proclaim it faithfully.

Jonah obeys

We are told in verse 3 that 'Jonah obeyed the word of the Lord and went to Nineveh.' As we have seen, obedience is the key to effectiveness. It is a difficult road to follow; there will be problems. But if we obey, God will use us and lead us to victory.

The tremendous way God delivered Jonah would have given him courage to be obedient. The experience of God's power would have made him confident in launching out on this difficult call. If God could rescue him from the raging seas, he would certainly sustain him in this wicked city.

Each experience of God's provision gives us strength for fresh exploits for God. In fact, it places on us the responsibility to launch out into new depths of obedience. Jonah's salvation from the seas was a blessing. Jonah's call to go to Nineveh was a commission.

Often blessings open doors to commissions. Have you seen God work in your life? Have you seen him answer prayer? Have you seen him guide you through turbulent times? Have you experienced his healing touch on your body? Then if he gives you some new assignment, take heart and follow. The blessing gives us the courage to be obedient.

Preaching judgment in Nineveh

In verse 3 the author adds a note about the importance of Nineveh: 'Now Nineveh was a very important city – a visit required three days.' The New American Standard is more literal. It says, 'Nineveh was an exceedingly great city, a three day's walk.' This statement has provided some material for those who deny the historical reliability of Jonah. Archaeology has revealed that the inner wall of Nineveh was about eight miles long. So why does the author say a visit required three days? Jonah could have completed the trip in much less than a day.

Perhaps the author meant it took three days to walk through the whole city, or that it took three days to cover the whole administrative district of Nineveh – greater Nineveh. Donald Robinson, who is now the Anglican Archbishop of Sydney and the author of the commentary on Jonah in the New Bible Commentary, points out that the entire circuit of the Nineveh district was sixty-one and a half miles, which would amount to a three days' journey.

'On the first day,' verse 4 tells us, 'Jonah started into the city. He proclaimed: "Forty more days and Nineveh will be overturned."' Starting to preach must have been very difficult. Jonah did not overcome this difficulty by secretly entering the city at night and whispering the message to a few people. We are told that he cried out, he proclaimed. The word suggests a bold proclamation. But once the start was made, the first big hurdle overcome, the news seems to have spread like wild fire. These people who had already been prepared by God came in crowds to hear him.

Let me mention in passing that the same thing happens when we witness to strangers. Often the hardest step is the first one. Very often when I'm travelling in a bus or a train, I know I should talk to the person next to me about Jesus Christ. Getting started is the hardest thing. My heart starts making all sorts of noises, and it is very difficult to begin. But once I've begun, I'm often surprised to see how open people are to the gospel. This isn't always the case, but often you will find it to be true.

'Forty more days,' Jonah proclaimed, 'and Nineveh will be overturned.' Nineveh is given forty days. The word *forty* in the Bible is often associated with judgment and testing. Notice that Jonah's message is a message of judgment. He says, 'Nineveh is going to be overturned.' Here is a stranger from a small and relatively weak nation, and these are arrogant, powerful Assyrians. It seems quite inappropriate for

Jonah to preach judgment. Wouldn't it have been better for him to preach about how important these people were to God? Shouldn't he have told them how much they could achieve if only God were on their side? Wouldn't large crowds have come to hear him if only he had told them how good they were in the sight of God?

It's true that people are important to God. When they are related to him, the possibilities of grace are so big that we cannot even fathom what God can do through them. But first Jonah had to preach a more important message. The Ninevites were selfish people. Their wickedness had gone up before God. They were headed for judgment, and they needed to be told that. So Jonah preached judgment.

Hebrews 6:2 says eternal judgment is one of the basic foundations of Christianity. The writer says we must build on that foundation, but I wonder if we've even laid it! Some say you can preach about judgment to uptight fundamentalists. You can say, 'Some of you will go to hell!' and they will respond 'Amen, brother!' Others say you can preach about judgment to primitive people living under the fear of the spirits, but not to sophisticated intellectual audiences. But when Paul preached to the Athenians, who were the most sophisticated audience he ever preached to, he preached about judgment (Acts 17:31). His method was philosophical because they were intellectuals, but his message included judgment.

It is interesting that two of the most brilliant minds the western church produced in recent centuries spent a lot of time reflecting and writing about judgment and hell. I refer to that brilliant

American scholar, Jonathan Edwards, and to the great British lay theologian and apologist, C.S. Lewis.

People have brought dishonour to the message of judgment by the way they've preached on hell. They have been unwise, insensitive and disrespectful of their audience. Many have condescendingly dumped accusations at prostitutes and drunks in a way that was an insult to their humanity. In the Bible, judgment is preached not only to prostitutes – they already know they are lost – but also to sophisticated intellectuals who walk about with their noses up in the air. Yet it is done in a way that is appropriate to them, just as Paul did in Athens when he approached the issue of judgment philosophically.

Revival in Nineveh

The response of the Ninevites is surprising: verses 3–9 describe a revival! The word *revival* is used in many ways today. But the specialized use in church history is for a widespread religious awakening, where not one person but large numbers of people take God seriously, confess their sin and get right with God. Usually revival refers to Christians who are revived and then respond in outreach to non-Christians. In Nineveh, however, those who were revived did not know God.

Verse 3 tells us that the Ninevites believed God. Now many eminent commentators believe that Nineveh's repentance was incomplete. They say that because Jonah's message was incomplete, the Ninevites could not have known enough about the Lord to exercise saving faith. Perhaps Jonah's message was incomplete, or perhaps only the salient features of his message were mentioned. We do not know. I greatly respect the scholars who don't think these people were really converted, but it seems to me that a genuine conversion took place.

The first response mentioned is that they believed God (v. 5). Then we are told that they declared a fast and that all of them, from the greatest to the least, put on sackcloth.

Fasting is a sign of lamentation or sorrow over sin. It is a physical expression of the earnestness of people who are abasing themselves before God. When the Ninevites fasted, it revealed that they were serious about their problem.

Sackcloth was normally worn only by poor, by prisoners or by slaves. By putting on sackcloth, the Ninevites showed that they had become serious about sin. They realized that sin is not something to be trifled with. Repentance is not something cheap, and they refused to ignore the gravity of sin. We see here a real sorrow over sin, a frank admission of guilt.

These people accepted their guilt before God. Then we are told in verse 6 that the king also repented: 'When the news reached the king of Nineveh, he rose from his throne, took off his royal robes, covered himself with sackcloth and sat down in the dust.' The king's action, of course, is a real evidence of revival. Instead of sitting on the throne, he sits down in the dust. Instead of wearing his royal robes, he puts on sackcloth. Now this is most unexpected when we realize the power of kings in ancient times. They were absolute monarchs. They made the rules. They were the law. They had no constitution to bind them, no investigative reporters or photographers to hound them.

Today the situation is so different. But even today, often the last thing leaders will do is to admit they are wrong. They will deny the charge. They will put the blame on someone else. They will make life difficult for those who accuse them. They will erase tapes. And they will shred documents.

To accept one's faults, however, is the sign of a truly great leader. This is often considered to be a sign of weakness because of our warped sense of values. But for a Christian, God's glory and honour are the most important thing. Sin dishonours God, and when a Christian leader sins, he or she dishonours God. But when a person accepts responsibility for his sin, he upholds God's principles.

The king issued a proclamation in Nineveh. 'By the decree of the king and his nobles: Do not let any man or beast, herd or flock, taste anything; do not let them eat or drink. But let man and beast be covered with sackcloth' (3:7–8).

Here is an official rule, urging expressions of sorrow over sin. Revival has resulted in laws which are conducive to holiness. Indeed, you cannot legislate morality; it must be a choice made by individual people. But the laws of the nation can certainly make it easier for people to follow the path of righteousness.

Sometimes, by refusing to take a stand on moral issues, governments make available to people things which they find difficult to handle in their own strength. Pornography is a good example. We say people must be free to choose on these matters. But after counselling young people who have been enslaved to pornography, I can say that by allowing youth to be exposed to pornography, governments have not affirmed their freedom but have contributed to their enslavement. Young people are powerless to overcome the temptation, though they would like to. Governments have the responsibility to provide an environment conducive to holiness. This law of the king does that.

Note that even animals are included in this repentance. In 4:11 God proclaims his concern for animals as well as people. The book of Jonah presents animals as a significant part of the community of Nineveh.

Throughout history, revivals have contributed to increased concern for animals. Revival makes people become what God intends them to be – truly human. This in turn means they become humane in their behaviour towards animals. Proverbs 12:10 states: 'A righteous man cares for the needs of his animal.' Earle Cairns, in his fine book on the history of revivals called *An Endless Line of Splendor*, points out that the Royal Society for the Prevention of Cruelty to Animals (RSPCA) was founded by an Anglican minister, Arthur Broome, with aid from William Wilberforce and his friends. These men were key figures in the great revivals of the eighteenth and nineteenth centuries.

In the second part of the king's proclamation (v. 8), we see what is probably the heart of revival: 'Let everyone call urgently on God.' All the outward acts mentioned previously find their meaning in this sentence. The people did all these things because they were serious about God. And that is the heart of revival. When people are serious about God, they see how serious their sin is.

The word translated 'urgently' is more literally

translated in the older translations as 'mightily' (ASV, KJV). The root meaning of the Hebrew word is 'strength.' We are talking about a situation when people seek God with their whole being, when they will not allow anything to stand between them and God.

If the previous section of Jonah described the heart of revival, the next section gives the evidence. It says, 'Let them give up their evil ways and their violence.' The mourning for sin described in verses 5–7 is very important. But as Leslie Allen points out, it also could be 'a cultic show of penitence.' There must be a change in behaviour. I have seen people weep at meetings where there was particularly severe conviction of sin, but after a few weeks I realized that their weeping was induced more by the atmosphere in the meeting than by true inner conviction on their part. There was no long-term change in their behaviour.

The history of revival shows that when revival comes, people give up their evil ways. Bars and brothels often close down, either for lack of business or because the owners themselves are converted. For example, after revival hit Asbury College and Seminary, convicted students returned books they had stolen from the seminary bookstore.

People give up not only moral evil but also social evil. The abolition of slavery in England was a direct result of revived people who realized that slavery is incompatible with Christianity.

The Earl of Shaftesbury is a great example of spiritual revival resulting in a passion for social justice. He realized that in England the poor and weak had no hope of improving their lot. They were being exploited, but they did not have the strength to overcome their exploitation. Shaftesbury knew this was evil, so he decided to battle the evil by introducing legislation which protected the poor and the weak.

His first struggle was on behalf of the mentally ill. Then he had legislation passed which protected factory workers from exploitation, especially women and children. Next he worked to introduce rules against abuses of chimney sweeps. The Duke of Argyll said, 'The social reforms of the past century have not been due to a political party. They have been due to the influence, the character, the perseverance of one man. I refer of course to Lord Shaftesbury.'

Yet Lord Shaftesbury was passionately committed to evangelism. He said, 'All life is reduced to a transaction between the individual soul and the individual Saviour.' On another occasion he said, 'I believe that the remedy for all our distress is one of the simplest and one of the oldest; the sole sovereign remedy is to evangelize the people by telling them the story of the cross on every occasion and in every place. I believe with all my heart that Christ and he alone is the power of God unto salvation.'

Are you committed to Jesus? Are you committed to his principles? Then you must be committed to fighting all forms of evil, both personal and social.

Verse 8 singles out one particular form of evil – violence. How relevant today! Violence is one of the most influential forces in the world today. Violence takes place when an end is pursued with no regard for human life, human welfare and moral law. This, of course, is how the Assyrians achieved their ends.

143

Today many people think that this is the quickest way to get things done. Indeed, you may achieve a short-term goal.

But we know that violence begets violence. Martin Luther King, in his book *Strength to Love*, called this 'the chain reaction of evil, resulting in a downward spiral of destruction.' Coming from a country which has so much violence, I can say that we Christians must stand up against violence and refuse to condone it as a suitable way to achieve our ends, however just those ends may be.

The king's proclamation concludes by expressing the hope that through God's mercy judgment might be averted. Verse 9 states, 'Who knows? God may yet relent and with compassion turn from his fierce anger so that we will not perish.' The king does not claim to deserve forgiveness; he only hopes for mercy. And such alone receive mercy, as an old Puritan saying states: 'God has two thrones: one in highest heaven, and the other in the lowliest heart.'

Those who thrust themselves on the mercy of God do indeed receive mercy, which is what happens next: 'When God saw what they did and how they turned from their evil ways, he had compassion and did not bring upon them the destruction he had threatened' (v. 10).

The words *had compassion* (NIV) are perhaps more accurately translated as 'relented' or 'repented' in other versions. These words are used when God changes his intended course of action because people change their course of action. When the Ninevites repented, God also repented.

Faithful to our call

Jonah 3 has given us a description of revival. Jonah, the agent of revival, was not the greatest model of godliness. He was what someone has called 'a reluctant missionary'. But he was obedient. He was faithful to his call, and God used him mightily.

That is what we must be. We must pray for revival. We must do all God asks us to do. We must proclaim the Word of God. We must denounce sin. We must demonstrate the love of Christ by our lives. We do all these things knowing that God will act in the way he knows best. We leave the results to him and do all we know to do. D.L. Moody once said, 'Pray as if everything depended on God, and work as if everything depended on you.'

God will send revival when he knows the time is ripe for it. But one thing we can do is to make sure we are in a revived state and obeying God in everything. Our prayer should be: 'Lord send revival, and let it begin with me!'

God's concern for Nineveh (Jonah 4)

In Jonah 3 we saw the great revival in Nineveh. Revivals are a time of rejoicing. Psalm 85:6 says, 'Will you not revive us again, that your people may rejoice in you?' If God uses a preacher as an instrument of revival, the preacher is usually the one who is most elated. It brings a person deep joy to be the chosen instrument of God for a special task.

Chapter 4 begins with one of the most profound words in the Bible – 'But.' *But* always introduces a change in direction. It indicates that something unexpected has happened. There are glorious *buts* in Scripture, but this is an inglorious *but*. Verse 1 says, 'But Jonah was greatly displeased and became angry.' God has miraculously worked, but the instrument of God's action is angry.

Verse 2 continues, 'He prayed to the Lord.' What follows doesn't sound like a prayer. It's actually a complaint. But it's a complaint which takes the form of a prayer. In the Bible we often find great servants of God complaining directly to God. The Bible never glorifies these complaints nor even justifies them. In fact, the complainer is often rebuked, although the rebuke is sometimes very gentle. It is foolish to doubt God's wisdom and his sovereignty. But if we do doubt God's ways, it is best to face up to the reality of that doubt and go directly to God with our problem. That's what Jonah did. When we go to God with our anger, we give him an opportunity to respond to our questions.

God responded to Moses when he complained about the burdens of leadership (Nu. ch.11). He responded to Jeremiah when he complained about his loneliness (Je. ch.15). He responded to the psalmist Asaph when he complained about the prosperity of the wicked in contrast to his own failures (Ps. 73). He responded to Jonah when he complained about his theological problem. Each of these responses gives us deep insights into the ways of God, because God answers their complaints. So while we can fault Jonah for his attitude, we can at least commend him for his honesty and for expressing his doubt.

Some orthodox people are afraid to be honest about their doubts. They won't grapple with them but suppress them. But when you suppress your doubts, you often become intellectually defensive, stiff, superficial. Often you become unreal.

Jonah was honest about his doubts, and because God is supreme he was not intimidated by Jonah's doubt. In fact, God gave Jonah an answer that was a deep revelation of truth. The doubt opened the way to deeper knowledge.

A deep experience of God often comes from struggle. The reason there are so many shallow people today is because they have avoided struggle. They have opted for quick solutions. And because they have opted for quick solutions, they never find the deep truths of God. Those who face up to their doubts, who go to God with those doubts and who wrestle with him about them will emerge with a deeper and surer faith.

Rejecting God's mercy

Notice Jonah's prayer in verse 2: 'Oh Lord, is this not what I said when I was still at home? That is why I was so quick to flee to Tarshish.' Finally we discover the reason for Jonah's disobedience in chapter one. Why did he flee to Tarshish? Why is he angry now? 'I know that you are a gracious and compassionate God, slow to anger and abounding in love, a God who relents from sending calamity.' Jonah was revolting against God extending his mercy to Gentiles.

147

Jonah's prayer is based on a common Jewish creed which is often quoted in the Old Testament. (For example, it is found in Exodus 34:6–7). The key phrase in the creed is 'abounding in love.' The RSV translates it as 'steadfast love.' The NAS renders it as 'loving kindness.' This is one of the most beautiful words in the whole Bible. The Hebrew word is *hesed*, which is often used to describe God's covenant love with Israel.

The word emphasizes God's *loyalty* to Israel. It stresses that he will be faithful to his covenant. But many Jews regarded *hesed* as a privilege reserved only for them. They did not want God to extend it to others. When God asked Jonah to go to Nineveh, he suddenly realized that God intended to show his *hesed* to the Gentiles. Jonah thought that *hesed* should only be given to those that deserve it. And the Jews, according to Jonah's way of thinking, deserved this loyal love of God.

But in the Bible the word *hesed* is very closely linked with mercy. In fact, the AV translates *hesed* as 'mercy' most of the time. Because God is merciful, he extends his covenant love to Israel. They don't deserve it. They don't merit salvation. God in his mercy has reached out to them. But when God reaches out to the Ninevites, Jonah revolts.

He is guilty of theological racism. I come from a country torn by racism, and I have observed that racism is one of the last areas the process of sanctification touches in many people's lives. It is shocking to see how many evangelical believers who say they're not racist have feelings of ill-will toward those of other races and view them as inferior. That is racism.

What was the reason for Jonah's theological racism? He had forgotten mercy. He had forgotten that he did not deserve salvation. Ephesians 2:8 puts this beautifully. 'It is by grace you have been saved, through faith – and this not from yourselves, it is the gift of God.' In Romans and Galatians, Paul is at pains to show that even in the Old Testament salvation was by grace. Nobody deserved salvation. Grace is God's free gift, and faith is acceptance of that gift. We don't have to do anything for our salvation except to repent and accept him as Saviour and Lord. So often people claim that other things are necessary for salvation – baptism or circumcision or whatever. But they are misinterpreting the Scriptures.

Jonah thought that the Jews deserved their salvation and the Ninevites did not. But Paul goes on to say in Ephesians 2:9 that it is 'not by works, so that no one can boast.' When people try to earn their salvation, they have an occasion for boasting. They think they are more deserving than others. So when so-called terrible sinners receive salvation, they say, 'That's not fair!'

That is how the elder brother responded to the prodigal son. He was angry like Jonah was angry. When the father questioned him about his anger, he said: 'All these years I've been slaving for you and never disobeyed your orders' (Lk. 15:29). His was a works-righteousness. He didn't know the joy of sonship. All he knew was the drudgery of slavery. People like that are very insecure about their salvation because deep down they know they can't save themselves. They have to keep comparing themselves with others to feel that they are all right.

149

So someone who understands that grace is not like that says, 'I don't deserve to be saved, but God showed me mercy. Praise God!' That's how Paul felt. In 1 Timothy 1:15–16 he says, 'Christ Jesus came into the world to save sinners – of whom I am the worst. But for that very reason I was shown mercy.' After contemplating God's mercy, Paul gets so excited that he bursts forth into praise to God: 'To the King eternal, immortal, invisible, the only God, be honour and glory for ever and ever. Amen.' He was so thrilled that Jesus had showed him mercy!

When we understand grace, our hearts overflow with thanksgiving. Grace also results in the love of God flooding into our hearts. This combination of thanksgiving and love flooding into our hearts bursts forth in evangelism. We are so grateful that we want others to know about God. Christ's love in us drives us and compels us to tell others about the salvation we have.

Jonah was wrong in thinking the Jews merited salvation. But he was also wrong in thinking that the Ninevites did not deserve God's mercy. This attitude is common even today. Often we regard people we dislike as unworthy of salvation. In our Youth for Christ ministry in Sri Lanka, much of our work has been with poor people. The hardest group we have tried to reach is the urban slum dwellers. These people have a lot of common vices, so they are disdained by society. (The vices of the rich are far more subtle, but they are just as abhorrent to God.) It has been very hard working with these people. We've seen a lot of failure, disappointment, heart-aches, betrayal and dishonesty. Many people have told us that these are dishonourable people, and it's no use working with them. The implication is that they don't deserve salvation.

I believe there is a similar situation among those working with the urban poor in the West. A Christian leader once told me he can't get money from certain foundations for work they do with the urban poor. He found it was easier to get funds for work with middle-class or rich people. The implication is that the urban poor are not worth spending so much money and energy on. You get quicker results with middle-class people.

The best answer we can give to that attitude is found in Romans 5:8, 'God demonstrates his own love for us in this: While we were still sinners, Christ died for us.' God didn't wait until we became worthy of salvation, because he knew that we didn't have the ability to become worthy. So Christ died for us so that we might be saved. Now that we have experienced salvation, we refuse to say that anyone is beyond salvation, whether they are rich or poor, black or white, yellow or brown. Whether they live in a mansion or in a ghetto, whether their lifestyle is that of a socialite or a violent criminal, they are all within the reach of grace. All can be saved, because grace comes through mercy. Such thinking was foreign to Jonah, so he complained about God showing mercy to the wicked Ninevites.

Jonah wants to die

Jonah's statement in verse 3 gives us a bigger shock. He prays, 'Now O Lord, take away my life, for it is better for me to die than to live.' He wants to die. This is the despair of a person whose theology is correct or orthodox, but whose personal desires clash with what he knows to be the will of God. In Hebrew, the words *I, me* and *my* appear nine times in verses 2 and 3. Jonah had the right theology, but he was self-centred. His selfishness caused his attitudes to be warped. His heart and his head were at logger-heads. His heart said, 'I and my people are better than other people because we deserve to be saved.' His head said, 'Salvation is an unmerited gift given because of God's mercy, and so the Ninevites need to hear it just like the Israelites.'

There was a conflict within him. He had lost his peace, that *shalom* which the Bible presents as the glorious heritage of those who belong to God. When those who are orthodox disobey God, they are some-times more miserable than those who don't know the truth. The orthodox know how powerful God is. They know they can't fight him, but in their heart they don't want to follow his ways. What a desperate situation to be in – to know the truth and still not want to follow it, to know the terrible danger of being opposed to God and still not want to agree with him. Such a conflict sometimes becomes so unbearable you come to the point where you think it would be better to die than to live. You become suicidal. And suicide is the ultimate expression of despair.

The Lord replies to Jonah, 'Have you any right to be angry?' The word translated as 'right' is closely related to the word *better* in verse 3. Both words have the idea of 'good.' Jonah says, 'It is good for me to die.' The Lord replies, 'Is it good for you to be angry?' Of course, neither is good. In a gentle way, the Lord questions and condemns Jonah's attitude.

The growth and destruction of the vine

Verse 5 says, 'Jonah went out and sat down at a point east of the city. There he made himself a shelter, sat in its shade and waited to see what would happen to the city.' This shelter must have been quite a temporary shelter, probably made out of branches and leaves that Jonah found there. It was obviously inadequate, because he was quite unhappy until God provided him with a vine.

We are told that Jonah sat and waited to see what would happen to the city. Why does he do this? Was he still hoping that God would judge and destroy Nineveh? Was he still waiting for some action from God which would explain his ways more clearly? We are not told the answers to those questions.

Verse 6 tells us that 'the Lord God provided a vine and made it grow up over Jonah to give shade to his head to ease his discomfort.' The word *provided* appears many times in this book. It's the same word which is found in 1:17, which says God *provided* a fish to save Jonah. Now he *provides* a vine to make him comfortable.

What is this plant? Verse 10 says it sprang up overnight. This may be literally true, in which case a miracle has taken place. Or the mention of it springing up overnight may be the figure of speech we call a hyperbole. If so, it is a way of describing rapid growth. Some have identified this vine as a *Ricinus communis*, the castor oil plant which grows very fast – but we can't be sure.

Verse 6 tells us that 'Jonah was very happy about the vine.' This is a very strong response. The NIV is a bit mild here. Leslie Allen translates it as 'terribly pleased.' The NASB has 'extremely happy.' In Hebrew the same adverb is used here as in verse one. So in verse 1 Jonah is 'terribly upset.' In verse 6 he is 'terribly pleased.' Jonah is having a roller-coaster type of emotional response. He is terribly upset when the Gentiles are saved and terribly pleased when he is looked after.

Why such extreme reactions? My beloved teacher, Daniel Fuller, said: 'Jonah regarded (the vine) as an acknowledgment of his inherent worth.' When the vine came up, Jonah seemed to say: 'I deserve God's help. Here is the evidence that God loves me. This is the way he should treat me.' But those trusting in themselves, who think they have inherent worth, are trusting in something very insecure. When they feel affirmed, they respond with great joy. But when they see others affirmed, they cry out 'Not fair!' like the brother of the prodigal son.

Two girls were walking along the street one day, and someone met them on the way, coming from the opposite direction. The person looked at one of the girls and said, 'You look very beautiful today.' The other girl was immediately baptized with a lemon-juice smile. For the rest of the day she was a sour-puss because her friend was affirmed and she was not.

Jonah's extreme reactions show the insecurity of one whose confidence and trust is in himself and not God. Those who trust in God have a quiet confidence, for their hope is not based on their abilities but on God's mercy and care. Isaiah 26:3–4 says, 'You will keep in perfect peace him whose mind is steadfast, because he trusts in you. Trust in the Lord forever, for the Lord, the Lord, is the Rock eternal.'

Jonah's joy is short-lived. Verse 7 says that at

dawn the next day God provided a worm that chewed the vine so that it withered. What is happening here? Suddenly a vine comes up, and suddenly it withers. God is using a method called the acted parable to get through to Jonah. Sometimes people are so hardened to truth that God can only get through to them by an unusual means.

God did this often in the Old Testament. Once he got a prophet to take a pot and walk around the city. The people thought this was very strange, so they all followed him. When the crowd had all gathered around him, they would not listen to his preaching, so the Lord asked the prophet to take the pot and throw it to the ground. He did so and said, 'That's what God is going to do if you don't repent.' They would not listen, and so God had to use an acted parable.

Again we find this same word *provide* in verse 7. In 1:17 God provided a fish to save Jonah. In 4:6 God provided a vine to shelter Jonah. Now God provides a worm to discipline Jonah and to teach him a lesson through the extreme discomfort he will shortly have to endure.

These uses of the word *provide* are related to a key theme of this book – God's holy love. God is both loving and holy. He not only blesses people with what they regard as good things. Sometimes God blesses people with chastisement or discipline. He allows us to experience discomfort, pain or heartache to teach us a lesson or to burn off impurities in our lives.

Discipline is one of the clearest examples of God's holy love. Proverbs 3:12 says, 'The Lord disciplines those he loves, as a father the son he delights in.'

Hebrews 12:6 also quotes that verse with approval. 1 John 4:8 says 'God is love.' But this love is not a weak, sentimental, soft love. It is holy love, tough love. Verse 8 presents God's discipline of Jonah at its peak when it says, 'When the sun rose, God provided a scorching east wind' – again the word *provided* – 'a scorching east wind, and the sun blazed on Jonah's head so that he grew faint.'

A recently published book called *The World of the Bible* describes what this scorching east wind is like. It is a dry, hot, desert wind called a sirocco that usually lasts for three to seven days. Normally the humidity of the Middle East is very, very low – forty to seventy-five per cent. During a sirocco, it can drop a further thirty per cent, so it becomes extremely dry. With that drop in humidity also comes a rise in temperature. The air is full of fine dust which blurs the sun, and the dryness makes it wearisome and unbearable. Dennis Bailey says, 'It is very trying to the temper and tends to make even the mildest of people irritable and fretful and ready to snap at one another for apparently no reason at all.' This is what Jonah had to encounter.

Normally when a sirocco comes people run for shelter. But Jonah's shelter is gone. The only place he could go was back to Nineveh – but he was not about to return there! His situation is desperate. He gets very weak, and we are told that he grows faint. In verse 8 we read that Jonah 'wanted to die, and said, "It would be better for me to die than to live".' He is totally defeated. Earlier he wanted to die because God had treated Gentiles the way he expected God to treat the Israelites. Now he wants to die because God is treating him the way he expects God

156

to treat the Gentiles. You can imagine Jonah's frustration! He has a stubborn heart, and God is trying to reach out to him. Jonah is brought to the end of himself before he is taught the great lesson of this book.

God expresses concern for Nineveh

God questions Jonah again, as he did in verse 4: 'But God said to Jonah, "Do you have a right to be angry about the vine?" "I do." he said. "I'm angry enough to die."' Jonah is snapping back at God. But God's answer is so typical of God. He does not rebuke the prophet for his attitude. He knows how much Jonah can handle. So instead of rebuking him, he gently but firmly begins to reason with Jonah.

This gentle firmness is seen very often in the Bible when God speaks to his discouraged servants. We see it in God's dealings with Moses, Jeremiah and Elijah when they complained. God disciplines us, but he does so wisely. He knows how much we can take and what's best for us. He never lowers his standards with us. But he varies his tone without varying his demands.

In verse 10 the Lord says, 'You have been concerned about this vine, although you did not tend it or make it grow. It sprang up overnight and died overnight.' God wants to stress to Jonah that he had no deep tie with the vine which withered. He did nothing for it. 'He had no investment' in it, as Kohlenberger says. It came up suddenly and died suddenly. Yet Jonah seems to be concerned for this vine.

God then goes on to say that his relationship with Nineveh is far more serious than Jonah's relationship with the vine: 'But Nineveh has more than a

157

hundred and twenty thousand people who cannot tell their right hand from their left, and many cattle as well. Should I not be concerned about that great city?' God describes the Ninevites as a people in need. They cannot tell their right hand from their left. That is, they don't know the truth. They don't know where to go. They are not innocent, but they are ignorant. God is concerned for them, not because of their inherent worth but because of their need.

Because they are needy people, God responds with concern and asks, 'Should I not be concerned about that great city?' The word that the NIV translates as 'concerned' has the idea of compassion or pity. The emphasis is on the helplessness of the Ninevites. This brings us to the heart of the gospel. We are helpless, under the power of sin. We have no hope, no ability to save ourselves. But God looked down on us in mercy and provided a way for our salvation.

Have you been saved? Then you know God is a compassionate God. If God is compassionate, there is hope for everyone. And if there is hope for everyone, you should be involved in proclaiming the gospel to those who don't know about it. God is a missionary God. His followers, therefore, must be missionary people.

This is one of the great arguments for missions. Robert E. Speer, the great lay missionary leader of the Presbyterian church in this country, said: 'The supreme arguments for missions are not found in specific words. It is in the very being and character of God that the deepest ground of the missionary enterprise is to be found. We cannot think of God except in terms which necessitate the missionary idea.' God is concerned for the lost. People are in need, and we are God's instruments. We must flesh out God's concern by our own involvement. Henry Martyn, who is one of my heroes, put it beautifully: 'The spirit of Christ is the spirit of missions. The nearer we get to him the more intensely missionary we must become.'

The Book of Jonah ends without telling us Jonah's response to God's teaching. That is an appropriate way to end this study. You, too, have been faced with the missionary challenge. Will you be an agent of God's concern for the lost? Will you give your life for it? If so, you will begin to share God's concern. And when you share God's concern, your heart begins to beat with the heartbeat of God.

Ajith Fernando, author, national director of Youth for Christ in Sri Lanka and a member of the Lausanne Committee for World Evangelization, has an international expository ministry.